Ending the Iraq War

A Primer

Phyllis Bennis

OLIVE
BRANCH
PRESS

An imprint of Interlink Publishing Group, Inc.
www.interlinkbooks.com

First published in 2009 by

OLIVE BRANCH PRESS
An imprint of Interlink Publishing Group, Inc.
46 Crosby Street, Northampton, Massachusetts 01060
www.interlinkbooks.com

Library of Congress Cataloging-in-Publication Data
Bennis, Phyllis.
Ending the Iraq war : a primer / by Phyllis Bennis. —1st ed.
p. cm.
Includes bibliographical references.
ISBN 978-1-56656-717-6 (pbk.)
1. Iraq War, 2003– —Evaluation. 2. Iraq War, 2003– —Influence.
3. United States—Politics and government—2001– I. Title.
DS79.76.B46 2008
956.7044'3—dc22

2008022255

Book design by Juliana Spear
Cover image by AP WideWorld Photos

Printed and bound in the United States of America
10 9 8 7 6 5 4 3 2 1

To request our complete 40-page full-color catalog,
please call us toll free at 1-800-238-LINK, visit our website at
www.interlinkbooks.com or write to Interlink Publishing
46 Crosby Street, Northampton, MA 01060
e-mail: info@interlinkbooks.com

R0429913224

TABLE OF CONTENTS

Preface ix

In the spring of 2008, a team of strategic analysts inside the Pentagon admitted what so many around the world have long understood. The US occupation of Iraq, said the report of the National Institute for Strategic Studies, "has achieved the status of a major war and a major debacle." It went on to describe the serious political costs the war has brought to the US, including how US standing in the world has seriously diminished. The report described how US actions in Iraq have created "an incubator for terrorism and have emboldened Iran to expand its influence throughout the Middle East."

Examining what was then five years of occupation, the Pentagon strategists were pessimistic about the future: "The outcome of the war is in doubt. Strong majorities of both Iraqis and Americans favor some sort of US withdrawal." Ultimately, the report's primary author concluded, "For many analysts (including this one), Iraq remains a 'must win,' but for many others… it now looks like a 'can't win.'"

More than five years after the beginning of the US occupation, and after more than six years of sustained antiwar mobilizations across the United States and around the world, the war in Iraq continues. As of July 23, 2008, more than one million US troops have served in Iraq: according to the Joint Chiefs of Staff, on that date the total reached 1,030,169 men and women.[1] More than a million Iraqis have been killed by the war and untold numbers injured; almost five million Iraqis are either refugees seeking safety outside their country or internally displaced from their homes. Iraq is a shattered country. With more than 4,000 US troops and more than 175 British troops killed, with the cost of the war to the US approaching $3 *trillion*, and hundreds of thousands of young soldiers returning from Iraq with grievous physical and mental injuries, the Iraq war is an unmitigated disaster.

Huge majorities—more than two-thirds—of the American and British people oppose the war. Around the world, even higher percentages demand an end to the occupation. But the US government led by George W. Bush, driven by ideology and deaf to both public outrage and the sober assessments of its own experts, remained unmoved. The war continues. Certainly the huge antiwar and anti-Bush majority anchored the popularity of 2008 Democratic Party candidate Barack Obama, who said he would end the war and called for pulling combat troops out of Iraq. But despite the enormous differences between his positions and those of his "stay-the-course" Republican challenger John McCain, neither candidate reflected the public demand for a real end to the US occupation of Iraq—which requires bringing home *all* the troops and mercenaries, closing *all* US military bases, and ending *all* efforts to control Iraqi oil.

While the antiwar movement has won the battle for public opinion, the public's views are often uncertain, not grounded in real information; antiwar opinion is wide but not deep enough. We need to continue our work, to escalate and educate, to provoke more and deeper opposition, more outrage, more demands for accountability.

This primer is indebted to the research of the committed Institute for Policy Studies Iraq Team, particularly Farrah Hassen, IPS's Newman Fellow. It is designed to answer the most "frequently asked questions" about how to end the war, and to serve as a resource for all citizens, US and global, and all policymakers working for peace and an end to the US–UK occupation of Iraq. It is long past time.

———PART I———

THE WAR IN IRAQ

What does Iraq at war look like?

Iraq is a devastated country. Its social fabric had already been ravaged by more than a decade of crippling economic sanctions before the 2003 US–UK invasion. Now after years of occupation and war, violence remains shockingly endemic. Iraqi civilians are killed in attacks by both foreign occupation forces and Iraqi resistance forces. Violence is carried out both by and against the US-installed Iraqi govern-ment's military and police forces, as well as by and against the various militias, many of them, on all sides of the religious divides, armed by the US. Sectarian violence rages within and between Iraq's disparate communities.

Iraq under occupation has no real democracy. It is "governed" by an elected president, parliament, and cabinet, but real power—economic, political, and military—lies with the occupying forces. With many parliamentarians living outside the country because of security concerns, the elected parliament can rarely manage a quorum; when it does, the US-allied government sequestered in the US-controlled "Green Zone" of Baghdad routinely ignores parliamentary decisions, to say nothing of public opinion.

Iraq has the potential to be a wealthy country, but after five years of US occupation even the capital city averages only two hours a day of electricity. Unemployment is rampant, and fear, violence, and desperation have caused more than 2 million refugees to flee the country, according to the UN High

Commissioner for Refugees. Another 2.7 million people are internally displaced, having fled their homes within Iraq. In August 2007, 60 percent of Iraqis described their lives as "bad" or "very bad."[2] That was six months into the US troop increase known as the "surge," which was ostensibly designed to create enough security for the Iraqi government to provide order and services for its people.

Didn't the "surge" strategy work?

The violence in Iraq, already terrible, spiked to an even greater intensity following the attack that shattered the Askariya shrine, the Golden Dome Mosque sacred to Iraqi Shi'a, in Samarra in February 2006. Sectarian violence in particular increased to unprecedented levels, as Shi'a communities and militias exploded with rage, which led to an escalation of retaliatory violence as well.

The violence continued to rise as the November 2006 US election campaign season got underway. By the end of the year, and following the massive defeat of Bush's Republican Party in the congressional election, the White House recognized that it needed to appear to respond to the continuing bloodbath. In January 2007 Bush appointed a new military chief in Iraq, General David Petraeus, who would emerge as a key supporter of administration policies of indefinite occupation and deployment of US troops. Petraeus was the primary author of the new Pentagon handbook on counterinsurgency war, and he took command of a troop "surge" strategy supposedly aimed at prioritizing the protection of Iraqi civilians. What the strategy did was send 30,000 additional US combat troops to Iraq. What it did *not* do was stop the killing of Iraqi civilians.

The dire rate of civilian deaths continued throughout 2006 and into 2007. By late May, the new Democratic-led Congress voted, as all the Republican-dominated Congresses before it had, to support the Bush administration's latest $100 billion supplemental funding bill for the war—and again refused to impose any conditionalities on the funding, any timetable for withdrawing troops, any strategy for ending the war. In June, as the violence was finally declining, especially against US occupation troops, Petraeus claimed that Baghdad was showing "astonishing signs of normalcy," although in fact the level of violence, primarily against Iraqi civilians, while lower, was still shockingly high.

General Petraeus released interim reports in July and early September, and, with US Ambassador to Iraq Ryan Crocker, delivered his congressionally mandated report to Congress on September 10, 2007. Opposition to the war was on the rise, and there was widespread public concern that the ambitious general—who had had Bush's ear from the beginning, even more than his nominal superiors in the military chain of command—would shape his report around White House preferences and priorities. Three weeks before his report was to be brought to Congress, the *Los Angeles Times* reported that "administration officials said it would actually be written by the White House, with inputs from officials throughout the government."[3]

The September 2007 Petraeus report did indeed reflect just what the White House wanted: the general testified that the troop surge was working and that "the military objectives of the surge are, in large measure, being met." He announced that a "drawdown" of the surge troops could bring troop numbers back to pre-surge levels by July 2008, but he cautioned against "rushing to failure," claiming that too rapid a troop withdrawal could reverse what he called progress.

There were three big problems with Petraeus's report. First, the reduction in violence itself was significant only in relative terms; Iraq remained a shockingly war-torn land. Second, the ostensible goal of the surge had been to reduce the level of violence in order to allow Iraq's feeble, occupation-backed government to meet a set of US-established political benchmarks. That goal hadn't come close to fruition. Third, and perhaps most significant in assessing Petraeus's claim of "success," his assertion that the reduction in violence was the result of the troop surge minimized, and at times even ignored, the major importance of three other factors taking place in Iraq during the same period.

Those factors included the unilaterally declared ceasefire of the fiery anti-occupation cleric Moqtada al-Sadr and his Mahdi Army militia. Another was the creation of the so-called Awakening Councils of largely Sunni fighters, some linked to the organization known as al-Qaeda in Iraq and others to various anti-occupation resistance organizations, all of whom agreed, at least for a while, to accept US cash payments in lieu of targeting US–UK occupation troops and the Iraqi government and military. And finally there was the horrific reality that much of the sectarian violence had ended because it had accomplished its bloody purpose: forcing residents of once mixed, heterogeneous neighborhoods, especially in Baghdad, into ethnically cleansed enclaves of all Sunnis, or all Shi'a, behind the twelve- or eighteen-foot-tall cement walls that separate sectarian micro-territories across the city.

All these factors had as much, or more, to do with the reduction of violence than the surge did. And none were created by or under the control of the US military. At any moment Sadr could revoke his ceasefire (as he had partially and temporarily in March 2008 in Basra). At any moment "Awakening Councils" might decide that the $300 a month they were being paid by the Pentagon could be matched or bettered by another militia group—and they could then return to fighting the occupation. And claiming a victory based on a successful ethnic cleansing is pretty dicey under any circumstances.

Congress was less than impressed. Democratic Representative Robert Wexler of Florida accused

Petraeus of "cherry-picking statistics" and "massaging information." But there was little serious challenge to the the Petraeus report or its consequences. Within three days after the high-profile congressional hearing, the media had largely agreed that Bush and the Democratic Congress were essentially "compromising." The *New York Times* headline was "Bush to Sell Limited Iraq Pullout as Middle Way," while the *Washington Post* featured "Democrats Push toward Middle on Iraq Policy."

By November 2007, just two months after Petraeus's appearance before Congress, the violence in Iraq had stopped declining and had leveled off. It stayed at more or less the same level until March 2008, when it spiked again. At that time, the Iraqi government, with US military support, attacked Sadr's militia in Basra, in the oil-rich region of southern Iraq, largely hoping to undermine Sadr's political forces in the run-up to the planned 2008 provincial elections. But Prime Minister Maliki, who led a competing Shi'a political party, failed to weaken Sadr's influence. Maliki's own forces couldn't hold their own, and over 1,200 Iraqi government soldiers and police refused to fight altogether, many of them defecting to Sadr's side. The fighting was fierce, as Sadr had given his militia leeway to fight in self-defense, while maintaining his ceasefire on offensive operations. After a week or so, Iran stepped in to orchestrate a ceasefire between the two Shi'a forces.

In the immediate aftermath of the Basra debacle, Petraeus and Crocker returned to Congress with their April 2008 surge report. The key claims were virtually unchanged from six months earlier: the "surge" was working, and US troops had to remain in Iraq. What was new was the much stronger focus on Iran as the strategic danger and the latest justification for why the US occupation of Iraq had to continue. As he had in his September testimony, Petraeus felt compelled to answer earlier charges that he was simply giving military cover to White House strategies, declaring again that he had written his testimony himself. On both occasions, he claimed that his report had not been cleared, shared, or approved ahead of time by anyone in the Pentagon or the White House. It wasn't clear who, if anyone, believed him. As the German newspaper *Der Spiegel* reported, "'I wrote this testimony myself,' Petraeus said, courteously but clearly, the model officer and gentleman. But the fact that the four-star general had to begin his testimony in this way indicates just how tense the atmosphere was."[4]

Isn't the Iraq war really a civil war between Iraqis?

The war that began with the US-led invasion of Iraq in 2003 has continued with several simultaneous wars being waged inside each other. But they all are rooted in the instability, chaos, and violence caused by the US invasion, and the civil wars will not end until the occupation has ended and US, British, "coalition," and private security forces are withdrawn.

The fighting began with a variety of resistance forces battling the US-led invasion. Their main target was the occupying military forces, as well as the US-controlled "Coalition Provisional Authority" that officially governed Iraq for the first years of the occupation. Soon the targets expanded beyond the occupation forces themselves, to include Iraqis perceived, accurately or not, as collaborating with the occupation.

The resistance was not limited to just one of Iraq's mosaic of ethnic/religious/linguistic communities (of which Shi'a Arabs, Sunni Arabs, and the primarily Sunni Kurds are the largest). But over time militias reflecting narrower sectarian interests were created both within and outside the largely disaggregated resistance movements. Sunni Arabs, who made up about 15–20 percent of the Iraqi population and had been disproportionately represented in the highest levels of the ruling Ba'ath Party and thus disproportionately privileged in access to wealth and power, have also been disproportionately represented in the resistance. Shi'a Arabs, the largest community in Iraq at 55–60 percent, were more divided, with some Shi'a leaders seeing the overthrow of the Ba'athist government as an opportunity for their community to seize and consolidate greater power within Iraq as a whole by accepting the terms set by the US–UK occupation. Other Shi'a resisted the occupation from the beginning, though some of them later shifted to a more acquiescent position. The Kurds, whose territory had been protected and whose leadership had been backed by the US throughout the pre-invasion years of brutal sanctions, were the most supportive of the US invasion from the beginning, seeing it as a way of consolidating their existing autonomy in the northern region of Iraq that they dominate. Throughout all these communities, many tried to maintain the kind of secular, nationalist identity that had long characterized Iraq's citizens, to whom "Iraqi" was a more important identity than Sunni, Shi'a, or even Kurd.

As the occupation tightened, and a sequence of US-backed Iraqi governments were installed and replaced, struggles for power among Iraqis became increasingly violent. Militias, some formally recognized and others unofficial and underground, were created to assert, protect, or attack sectarian community interests.

Outside forces joined the fray as well, with foreign fighters, the largest number apparently from Saudi Arabia, pouring into Iraq through suddenly porous borders. For many, the goal was not simply to oppose the US–UK occupation, but rather to impose a pan-Islamic ideology, characterized by some of the most extreme interpretations of Islam, on the people of Iraq—who had long been counted among the most secular peoples of the Arab world. While al-Qaeda in Iraq has likely been foreign-led from its beginning, increasing desperation rooted in long years of military occupation has led to increased involvement by Iraqis themselves, and the forces in and around al-Qaeda in Iraq have continued to attack occupation forces as well as carrying out terrorist attacks against civilians, primarily Shi'a.

From the beginning there has been significant overlap between the anti-occupation violence of the resistance and the rising sectarian violence carried out by some of those same militias and other forces. It is for this reason, along with an understandable level of fear, that many Iraqis have been less willing to challenge those who attack civilians—because those same attackers are also taking on the widely hated occupation forces.

What are the costs of the war for Iraq and Iraqis?

In the first weeks of the US-led invasion and occupation of Iraq, Pentagon officials on the ground and in Washington refused to quantify, analyze, or indeed even acknowledge the Iraqi victims of the war—the dead, the injured, those made refugees. As General Tommy Frank, then commander in Iraq, put it, "we don't do body counts."

But others do. The numbers of Iraqi civilians killed in the war are inexact, but the broad parameters— and the escalations—are clear. The Iraq Body Count, a British organization that tallies only those deaths identified in Iraqi or international media coverage, had documented 86,609–94,490 deaths by August 2008. In one of the most comprehensive studies, Johns Hopkins University and the British medical journal the *Lancet* placed the number of civilians who died because of the war at 655,000 as of fall 2006. Of those, over 600,000 were killed by violence. In the most recent study, including the period of the 2006–2007 spike in sectarian and other violence in Iraq that came after the *Lancet* survey was completed, the British ORB polling firm documented more than 1.2 million civilian deaths as of September 2007 by using household surveys across Iraq. As the London *Observer* described it, "the ORB survey follows an earlier report by the organization which suggested that one in four Iraqi adults had lost a family member to violence. The latest survey suggests that in Baghdad that number is as high as one in two. If true, these latest figures would suggest the death toll in Iraq now exceeds that of the Rwandan genocide in which about 800,000 died."[5] That survey was made public the same week that General David Petraeus, US commander in Iraq, reported to Congress on the alleged reduction in violence underway in Iraq because of the so-called surge.

There are no statistics available for the number of Iraqi civilians who have been grievously wounded and injured by the war. The *Lancet* study indicated that almost half of those Iraqi civilians killed in war-related violence were shot, with the other half killed by bombings, military raids, and other violent actions that create multiple casualties. So it can be assumed that about half of those killed—perhaps half of as many as 1.2 million—were killed in situations causing other injuries and casualties. The Pentagon has bragged that its state-of-the-art military medicine has reduced the injured-to-dead ratio for US soldiers in Iraq to one in seven—meaning that six out of seven injured soldiers survive. That is one of the very few pieces of good news for the US occupation troops. But there is nothing close to that level of medical assistance available to injured Iraqis—especially Iraqi civilians.

Violence under the US–UK occupation had become so dire by 2006 that huge numbers of Iraqis were forced to flee their homes. By spring 2008, more than 2 million had become refugees, most of them seeking safety in Jordan and Syria, as well as other countries. Another 2.7 million had become internally displaced persons—still living in Iraq, but forcibly expelled or frightened into leaving their homes, unable to return and either relying on friends or family for support and shelter or forced to turn to the informal refugee camps springing up around the country.

In April 2008, UNHCR, the United Nations' refugee agency, reported, "The plight of some 2.77 million internally displaced Iraqis remains precarious. ... According to the latest estimates, the number of IDPs in need of shelter and food now tops a million. More than 1 million internally displaced people have no regular income, and some 300,000 have no access to clean water. Tens of thousands are in need of legal aid to enable them to access other basic services." UNHCR also stated that it had received less than half the $261 million it had requested to address the situation.[6] The High Commissioner declared that "Iraqi refugees throughout the region have become increasingly desperate."

The UN has consistently maintained that conditions in Iraq remain so dangerous that Iraqi refugees should not return home to most of the country. While the US ($95 million) and the UK ($6.2 million) were the largest contributors to the UNHCR appeal for work on behalf of Iraqi refugees, those two countries most responsible for the war and the resulting creation of the refugee crisis have taken almost no responsibility for providing asylum to desperate Iraqis. In April 2008 the British government successfully fought against an Iraqi seeking asylum in the UK. The Home Office actually argued that there was no "internal armed conflict" in Iraq, and the Asylum and Immigration Tribunal's ruling accepted the government's arguments, and claimed that "Neither civilians in Iraq generally, nor civilians even in provinces and cities worst affected by the armed conflict, can show they face a 'serious and individual threat' to their 'life or person' ... merely by virtue of being civilians." The United Nations refugee office called the ruling a "sword of Damocles" held over Iraqis in the UK, saying "we strongly advise against the return of anyone to central or southern Iraq." According to the European Council for Refugees and

Exiles, only 13 percent of Iraqi asylum claims were approved in the UK in 2007, compared to 82 percent in Sweden and 85 percent in Germany. Only about 500 Iraqis were allowed to stay in the UK in all of 2007.[7]

The US treatment of Iraqi refugees has been just as disgraceful. In 2006 the US admitted only 202 Iraqi refugees—total.[8] The US government announced it would take 7,000 in fiscal 2007, still only a tiny percentage of those who had worked for the US occupation forces as translators or in other vulnerable positions and were now targeted by various anti-occupation forces. Then it reduced the 2007 goal to 2,000. By the end of that fiscal year even that embarrassingly low target remained out of reach. And the AP reported in early 2008 that "U.S. admissions of Iraqi refugees are nose-diving amid bureaucratic in-fighting."[9]

What do Iraqis want?

There is no question that Iraqis overwhelmingly want an end to the US occupation. In September 2006, the US State Department conducted a poll of Iraqi opinion that showed that almost 2/3 of Iraqis wanted an immediate withdrawal of all occupation forces. Iraqis told State Department pollsters that such a pullout would make the country more secure and would reduce the level of sectarian violence. Even more Iraqis, almost 3/4 of those polled, indicated that they would feel safer if the US and all other foreign forces left Iraq.

That kind of pull-out was in fact the campaign commitment made by most of the victorious parties in Iraq's elected parliament, but a commitment they overwhelmingly disavowed once they took office in the US-protected Green Zone. In fact the *Washington Post* article describing both polls, "Most Iraqis Favor Immediate U.S. Pullout, Polls Show," included a telling subtitle: "Leaders' Views Out of Step With Public."[10]

In September 2007, a poll conducted by the BBC, ABC Television, and the Japanese NHK network found comparable views—except that opposition to the US occupation was even stronger. The BBC reported their poll under the stark headline: "US Surge Has Failed: Iraqi Poll." At that time, months into the "surge" troop additions, only 21 percent of Iraqis supported the presence of US–UK forces in Iraq. Only 5 percent "strongly" supported the occupation troops, while 79 percent opposed their presence— with 53 percent "strongly" opposing. Another damning view was made clear in the same survey: 57 percent of Iraqis believed that military attacks on occupation forces were acceptable. In contrast, only 7 percent believed attacks on Iraqi government forces were acceptable.

It is perhaps even more significant that the trajectory of opinion over the years of war and occupation consistently shows diminishing support of and rising opposition to the presence of US–UK troops in Iraq, as the chart below illustrates.

> *Do you strongly support, somewhat support, somewhat oppose, or strongly oppose the presence of Coalition forces in Iraq?*
>
> In percentages:
>
> | | 2004 | 2005 | Feb '07 | Aug '07 |
> |---|---|---|---|---|
> | Strongly support | 13 | 13 | 6 | 5 |
> | Somewhat support | 26 | 19 | 16 | 16 |
> | Somewhat oppose | 20 | 21 | 32 | 26 |
> | Strongly oppose | 31 | 44 | 46 | 53 |
> | Refused/don't know | 10 | 3 | — | — |

It is noteworthy that in a similar poll conducted six months later, when overall violence in Iraq had significantly decreased, the changes in Iraqi public opinion were less dramatic than one might have expected. Those believing that the 2003 US–UK invasion of Iraq was absolutely or somewhat right rose from 37 percent to 49 percent, but those expressing either a "great deal" or "quite a lot" of confidence in the US occupation forces remained low, rising only 4 percent, from 16 percent to 20 percent. And those expressing either "not very much confidence" or "none at all" in the occupation forces dropped only 6 percent—remaining at a sky-high 79 percent.[11]

The polls also showed that the period of the "surge" matched a period of escalating demand for an immediate withdrawal of occupation forces. In February 2007, 35 percent of Iraqis wanted the US–UK troops out immediately. By September of that year, six months into the "surge," less than 10 percent supported the Bush administration's call for occupation troops to remain, and 47 percent of those surveyed now wanted the troops out immediately. And even in the specific areas of Iraq where "surge" troops were sent, almost 3/4 believed the new US troops had made the security situation worse.[12]

The "surge" did not build support for the US-led occupation. Confidence in the occupation forces had dropped from 19 percent in 2003 to 15 percent in August 2007; those with "not very much" confidence rose from 20 to 27 percent. And the percentage of those whose confidence level was "none at all" rose from 52 to 58.

When asked about the impact of the "surge" troop increase on the Iraqi government's ability to function, 65 percent in August 2007 said it made things worse. 67 percent said the pace of reconstruction was slower under the "surge"; 67 percent said the same about the pace of economic development.

Certainly there are other issues affecting life in Iraq today. People want jobs, security in the streets, reliable electricity and clean water, safer and better schools for their children. The 2.7 million Iraqis displaced within the country, mainly as a result of the ethnic cleansing of neighborhoods, want to return to their homes in safety and security. The 2 million Iraqi refugees, mainly in Syria, Jordan, and Iran, want security sufficient for them to return home as well—and in the meantime they want sufficient assistance and recognition and to be treated with dignity.

But most of all Iraqis want an end to occupation. While the pullout of US troops will not bring an immediate end to all the violence, the process of ending the violence cannot begin in earnest *until* the US, British, and "coalition" troops, as well as private security forces, are withdrawn.

Didn't Iraqis want the US to overthrow Saddam Hussein?

There is no doubt that Saddam Hussein's Ba'athist government was extremely repressive. Collective resistance—including several Kurdish uprisings and Kurdish collaboration with Iranian troops during the Iran–Iraq war, and later the 1991 Shi'a uprising first encouraged and then abandoned by the US—was repeatedly met with savage military responses. As is the case in many countries, including many Middle Eastern allies of the United States, political rights such as freedom of speech and assembly were largely curtailed, and severe punishment including arrest, imprisonment, torture, and assassination or execution faced anyone accused of disloyalty or organizing against the regime.

At the same time, most economic and social rights in Iraq were respected, and Iraq from the mid-1970s through the 1980s built a secular, largely middle-class society in which the gap between the rich and the poor was one of the smallest in the region. Even with the massive human and economic cost of the eight-year-long Iran–Iraq war, Iraq still provided free secular education for both boys and girls, including university and advanced study abroad, free health care in one of the most advanced medical systems in the Arab world, a wealthy and thriving private sector, and even widespread access to international travel. In fact, only months before the 1990 invasion of Kuwait, which triggered the 1991 Gulf War and subsequent years of devastating economic sanctions, UNICEF was about to shut down its Iraq operations and create an Iraqi Committee for UNICEF in which Iraqis would donate funds to support UNICEF's work in other, poorer countries, much as the US Committee for UNICEF does.

By the time of the March 2003 US-led invasion, the 1991 Gulf War and twelve years of sanctions had crippled Iraq's economy, and shredded intellectual life and the social fabric of the country. There had been several internal military efforts to replace Saddam Hussein, but they had all failed. Iraqis were desperate, and many undoubtedly hoped that some outside force would overthrow the oppressive dictatorship. But most Iraqis also remembered that for almost two decades Saddam Hussein's regime had been armed, financed, and politically supported by the United States, from CIA assistance in Hussein's consolidation of power in Iraq in the 1970s and 1980s through US arming of Iraq during the Iran–Iraq war, and only ending with Iraq's invasion of Kuwait in August 1990. Few Iraqis likely had confidence that the US would suddenly move to support Iraqi, rather than its own, interests.

The small cabal of exiled Iraqis who built close ties during the 1990s with a range of neoconservative and other US political forces certainly were eager for the US military to move decisively against Saddam Hussein's regime. The most prominent among them was Ahmad Chalabi, who had spent his adult life in comfortable exile in Lebanon, the UK, and the US, after secretly escaping Jordan where he had been convicted of massive bank fraud. Chalabi's goals had far more to do with personal empowerment and enrichment than with improving the lives of ordinary Iraqis.

For ordinary Iraqis, the abstract wish for an end to their repressive government in no way constituted a wish for the death and destruction wrought by the Pentagon's "shock and awe" campaign, let alone the extreme violence and displacement of the subsequent years of occupation. The war has not left Iraqis better off, and few Iraqis believe the war was launched or fought on their behalf at all.

Years after, when asked whether, all things considered, the 2003 invasion was ultimately right or wrong, the number of Iraqis who believed it was "absolutely right" dropped from 20 percent in 2004 to just 12 percent by August 2007. Those who believed it was wrong jumped from 39 percent in 2004 to 63 percent—almost two-thirds—by 2007. And 35 percent believed the invasion was "absolutely" wrong.[13]

Who are Iraq's Shi'a, Sunnis, and Kurds?

Unlike most of the modern Arab countries, which were created in 1922 when British and French colonialists drew lines on a map to divide the Middle Eastern spoils following the collapse of the Ottoman Empire, Iraq has a longstanding national identity rooted in its past as the ancient land of Mesopotamia.

The borders of Mesopotamia were not exactly the same as those assigned to Iraq at the end of World War I—what is now called Kuwait was long considered a part of Iraq; much of what is now Iraqi Kurdistan was not—but they were pretty close. So when contemporary Iraq was created, bringing together three distinct large (and numerous smaller) religious, ethnic, and linguistic communities, there was already a kind of national consciousness in place that took decades to develop in other countries. These communities—Shi'a and Sunni Arabs, the largely Sunni Kurds, as well as Christian and Jewish Arabs, Turkmans, mostly Shi'a Persians, and many more—inhabited the new nation of Iraq in different ways, some in longstanding identifiable enclaves but many more in large polyglot and heterogeneous cities and regions.

There was some social tension and discrimination among the various groups, but rarely any violence (although Iraq saw more than its share of general political violence over the years). Certainly, the government harshly repressed uprisings rooted in specific communities, such as the 1991 Shi'a uprising that followed the US Gulf War. Kurdish uprisings before and during the Iran–Iraq war, and Kurdish separatism in general, faced a long history of suppression. But relative to almost all the other Arab states, modern Iraq—possibly *because* of its heterogeneity—developed in a thoroughly secular manner. In contemporary Iraq, especially in Baghdad where almost a quarter of the country's population lives, mixed families—especially Sunni–Shi'a intermarriages—have been a common and familiar phenomenon for years.

The sectarian character of Iraq's post-occupation civil war has its origins in the explicitly sectarian policy of the US occupation. US strategy following the 2003 invasion was to establish an Iraqi government based on sectarian parties and leaders. During the years of Ba'ath Party rule in Iraq, members of the Sunni minority were disproportionately privileged in many government and military positions; but the government overall maintained a clearly secular nationalist approach. The US-created Iraqi Governing Council, in contrast, was designed explicitly to consolidate sectarian divisions in the country; its formal organizing principle assigned power based on each group's percentage of the Iraqi population according to a census taken years earlier. The same organizing principle shaped the elected Iraqi government formed under US occupation in 2005, in which almost all parties were based on the perceived communal interests of a particular sect.

The Shi'a

Iraq's Shi'a Arabs are the largest community—thought to number between 55 and 60 percent of the population. During the 400-year rule of the Ottoman Empire and the post–World War I rule of the British-installed Hashemite monarchy, Iraq's ruling elite was primarily composed of Sunni Arabs, though there was always a small Shi'a component within the powerful circles that controlled the country. But most Shi'a remained relatively poor and with less access to power. During the years of the Ba'ath Party's rule following the overthrow of the monarchy in 1958, the Shi'a made up the majority of the military (although the top brass were disproportionately Sunni).

The popular Shi'a uprising in 1991, at the end of the US Gulf War, was one of the first specifically Shi'a military resistance movements against the Iraqi government. President George H.W. Bush had encouraged and incited that rebellion, implying it would have US support. But when the uprising began, the US was already pulling its troops out of Iraq and abandoned the Shi'a to face the ruthless repression of Baghdad's military.

In the meantime, many of the Shi'a elite had gone into exile during the years of Saddam Hussein's rule. Some, such as the Pentagon favorite Ahmad Chalabi, made fortunes in other Arab countries or Europe (Chalabi himself also was convicted in Jordan of embezzlement and bank fraud that brought down a major Jordanian bank), and only returned to Iraq under Washington's protection during the 2003 US invasion and occupation. Iraqi Shi'a, particularly the elite, continue to dominate the Baghdad government installed under the protection of the US occupation. Shi'a parties control the prime minister's office as well as crucial economic and security ministries; for many Iraqis, the Iraqi army itself appears less a national military than a larger-than-usual Shi'a militia, one that happens to be under the control of Prime Minister Maliki's Dawa Party and its allies.

The Sunnis

In the French–British colonial trading schemes that drew borders for new countries across the Middle East, scions of the Sunni Sharif of Mecca in the Arabian peninsula, what would soon become Saudi Arabia, were placed on the thrones of the newly created countries of Transjordan, Syria, and Iraq. One of Sharif's sons, Faisal bin Hussein bin Ali, was briefly anointed king of French-controlled Syria. He was expelled by the French and was soon appointed by the British to become king of Iraq in 1921. Faisal's son and then grandson succeeded him, until his grandson Faisal II was overthrown in the revolution against the monarchy in 1958.

Throughout that period of British rule and influence, Iraq's Sunni minority (about 20 percent of the population) gained disproportionate economic and political power. The post-independence Ba'athist governments after 1958 were officially secular but relied on and rewarded the existing, largely Sunni, elite.

Sunnis were disproportionately (although far from exclusively) represented in the upper echelons of the Ba'ath Party itself, and they were the group for whom the US invasion and occupation caused the most direct and immediate loss of power and influence. This loss was caused particularly by the US decision to dissolve the Ba'ath Party and the Iraqi military, in both of which Sunnis were particularly powerful. Not surprisingly, from the beginning of the US–UK invasion, Sunnis were disproportionately (although, again, far from exclusively) represented in the resistance to the occupation.

The Kurds

Iraq's Kurds have a more consistent history of claiming a separate ethnic and linguistic identity than any other group in the country. Globally, the Kurds as a whole number about 30 million, and are often named the largest ethnic/national group in the world without a state of their own. In the Treaty of Sevres following World War I, the Kurds were promised their own state. But the post-Ottoman Turkish nationalist Kemal Ataturk claimed major Kurdish areas as part of the new nation of Turkey, and the US and its European allies, victors of the war, reneged as well. Instead of an independent Kurdistan, the territory was divided up largely according to European colonial imperatives. Divided by newly created borders,

Kurdistan became part of the new states of Turkey, Iran, Iraq, Syria, and Azerbaijan (itself then part of the Soviet Union). The borders of the new state of Iraq were drawn to include the Kurdish-majority Ottoman province of Mosul, largely because of the oil deposits Great Britain believed were there.

The Kurds have faced varying levels of discrimination under each of those governments, though by far the greatest consistent subjugation was in Turkey and Iraq. But throughout the region, and despite repressive responses, Kurds have sought to maintain an autonomous national life, including efforts to preserve the Kurdish language and to achieve some indigenous Kurdish control over their territory and society.

What is the special relationship between Iraqi Kurds and the US?

The US has a sordid history of embracing Kurdish leaders and claiming to support Kurdish aspirations, only to abandon both when tactical advantage requires otherwise. In 1975, while the US maintained close ties with the shah of Iran, then Secretary of State Henry Kissinger orchestrated a plan to provide $16 million in military aid to Iraqi Kurds to launch an uprising against Baghdad as a means of weakening Iraq and thus strengthening Iran. Great promises of support for Kurdish independence were made. But as soon as Iran and Iraq resolved their border dispute, the US pulled the plug on funding and abandoned the

Kurds, who were soon overrun by the Iraqi military. Reacting to a plea for help from the Kurdish leaders he had pretended to support, Kissinger told an assistant, "covert action should not be confused with missionary work."[14]

For most Kurds, US support or opposition to their national cause was determined by the US's relationship with the particular government under which they lived. For instance, demands for greater autonomy by Turkish Kurds, especially (but not only) those who supported the militant Kurdish Workers' Party or PKK, were always viewed with suspicion and even hostility by the US and its allies because of their close strategic alliance with Ankara. On the other hand, the US welcomed those same demands for Kurdish autonomy, even independence, by Iraqi Kurds under Saddam Hussein's regime after 1990, since the US was also opposed to the regime at this time.

Earlier, of course, the US view of the situation in Iraq had been quite the opposite. Saddam Hussein's government, always suspicious of Kurdish intentions, had made Iraqi Kurds a special target of repression. The *anfal* campaign in the 1980s aimed to force Kurds out of parts of their historic homeland and "Arabize" once-Kurdish villages. Illegal poison gas was used against the Iraqi Kurds as well as against Iranian troops during the Iran–Iraq war. None of that bothered the US government. The close relations between Washington and Baghdad, symbolized in the infamous 1983 photo of Saddam Hussein shaking hands with

Donald Rumsfeld, then a special envoy of Ronald Reagan eager to reestablish normal diplomatic and oil relations with Iraq, continued throughout the 1980s. As Washington embraced Iraq under Saddam Hussein, its pre-1975 support for Iraqi Kurds disappeared, despite Baghdad's *anfal* campaign and other attacks, and would not reappear until 1990 when Iraq invaded Kuwait and once again the US reversed its alliances.

At that time, the US turned against its former client, Saddam Hussein, and went to war against Iraq in January 1991. Washington re-embraced the Iraqi Kurds after Desert Storm, turning the northern Kurdish region of Iraq into a US–UK protectorate. So when the 1991 war was followed by more than a decade of international economic sanctions, and the US reengaged Iraq's Kurds as a partner against the now-demonized Saddam Hussein, US and British warplanes patrolled the skies above Iraqi Kurdistan, protecting the region from Baghdad's military reprisals. (The US, with the UK's support, created the "no-fly" zone, and President Clinton famously claimed that UN resolutions required the US to enforce the zone; in fact, no UN resolution ever even mentioned creation or enforcement of "no-fly" zones in Iraq.)

Iraqi Kurdistan's oil sales and trade with Turkey, only barely disguised despite the sanctions, flourished, and the Kurds kept their borders far more open than the sanctions allowed in the rest of Iraq. Abundant water and productive land meant less dependency on chemical fertilizers prohibited by the sanctions, and a complicated financial scheme resulted in people in Iraq's northern (Kurdish) region receiving dispro-portionately more revenue per capita from the oil-for-food plan. These and other factors allowed Iraqi Kurds to survive the devastation of the sanctions years in significantly better shape than the rest of the country. As a result, Kurdish civil society thrived and political parties were able to capitalize quickly on newly strengthened relations with Washington.

So when the US and the UK invaded Iraq in 2003, it was no surprise that the Kurds in northern Iraq quickly became the most pro-American of all of Iraq's communities and far less critical of the occupation than any other sector. Under US tutelage and support, Iraq's Kurds officially sidelined their longstanding demand for independence, concen-trating instead on trying to shape the Iraqi government so that maximum power would devolve to regional authorities. But US backers of the Iraqi Kurds continue to play the Kurdish independence card in the context of calls for dividing Iraq into three separate "countries." Iraq's Kurds have created a stronger regional government than any other province, have signed regional oil contracts with international oil companies, and play an influential— sometimes spoiler—role in the Iraqi parliament, particularly when it comes to determining whether the oil-rich city of Kirkuk belongs to the Kurdish northern region or the mixed central provinces.

Aren't there huge differences between Iraq's Sunnis, Shi'a, and Kurds? Shouldn't we just divide Iraq into three separate states?

As indicated in the question above, Iraq from its origins has been a heterogeneous country, with a wide mix of ethnicities, religions, sects, and languages. But for generations those differences, except perhaps in the case of Iraq's Kurds, were far less important than Iraqis' identity *as* Iraqis—the national identity remained primary. This was not a situation like that often attributed to the former Yugoslavia, in which many believe a powerful central government imposed an artificial national polity on reluctant small nations, each still attempting to maintain its own separate identity. Rather, contemporary Iraq had had a reputation from the earliest post–World War I division of the Ottoman Empire as one of the two most secular Arab countries (the other being Palestine). Although government repression was sometimes directed against a particular community (mostly Kurds, though on occasion various Shi'a groupings) within society, Iraqis who happened to be Sunni or Shi'a Muslims intermarried freely. Smaller contingents of Turkmans, Christians, Jews, and others tended to marry within their own groups, but intermarriage was not rare for them either, and the communities constantly intermixed in business, education, and social circles. Certainly identifiable communities with large concentrations of one or another ethnic or religious group existed: Iraqi Shi'a dominated the South, Turkmans were a large presence in Kirkuk, etc., but the large cities remained thoroughly mixed. Baghdad in particular, in which about a quarter of the entire Iraqi population lived, was notable for its cosmopolitan and diverse population and neighborhoods. On a national level, Sunnis were disproportionately wealthy, Shi'a disproportionately poorer—but in a country with one of the smallest gaps between wealth and poverty, and with a huge middle class, even those economic distinctions had less impact than would have otherwise been the case. Iraqi Arabs, Shi'a, Sunni, Jewish or Christian, Turkmans, Iraqi Kurds, despite speaking their own language as well as Arabic—all shared a national Iraqi identity.

From the beginning of the US-led invasion and throughout the occupation, US strategy has been based on undermining that national identity, and instead dividing Iraqis according to religion, sect, and ethnicity. Not surprisingly, the US encouraged the sect-based parties that had quickly risen to prominence under the US–UK occupation. So Sunni parties competed for power with each other (both for support from other Sunnis and for power in the national or regional or local governments), and Shi'a and Kurdish parties the same. From 2003 on, each community has included sectarian parties and leaders and many who follow a sectarian path, but each also has its share of non-sectarian, secular, Iraqi nationalist, and unitary forces.

More importantly, beyond any outsider's assessment of the relative strength of Iraqis' national vs. sectarian identities, there is a serious problem with US diplomats, Congress, military leaders, and other officials debating so blithely whether "we" shouldn't just divide Iraq into three parts. The notion of "we" choosing to divide—or unite—Iraq from outside is rooted in a set of thoroughly colonial assumptions about who has the "right" to impose their will on Iraq and Iraqis from outside.

The first line of Caesar's *The Gallic Wars* provides the classic validation of expansive, preventive war for empire: "All Gaul is divided into three parts." The question for US policy should not be whether "we" repeat Caesar's choice of how to establish an empire's control over Iraq, but rather how to empower Iraqis to rebuild their own country as they see fit. Only after the US–UK occupation has ended, with US, British, and "coalition" troops and mercenaries all withdrawn, will Iraqis be able to reclaim what now seems so out-of-reach: the ability to identify and isolate sectarian forces, remove them from power, and reunify their country. The US–UK invasion and the years of occupation set in motion a series of wars and conflicts inside Iraq, many of which have taken a brutally sectarian direction. The challenge of overcoming those divides, as well as the terrorism and campaigns of ethnic cleansing that accompanied them, will clearly be difficult for Iraq, and will remain perhaps the most bitter legacy of the US war.

Didn't the US bring democracy, a constitution, and an elected government to Iraq?

We own half the world, "oh say, can you see,"
And the name for our profit is Democracy
So like it or not you will have to be free,
'Cause we're the cops of the world, boys, we're the
cops of the world.
—"Cops of the World," Phil Ochs, 1965

When the original pretexts for the US invasion of Iraq in 2003 were proven false the Bush administration switched to another: democratization.

Among the proponents of this focus were those inordinately powerful US officials who maintained colonial-style visions of remaking the Middle East in the image of Western "market democracies." From the beginning these enthusiasts, led by Deputy Defense Secretary Paul Wolfowitz, had called on the Bush administration to openly assert "democratization" and "ending Saddam Hussein's human rights violations" as key legitimating motives for war.

These were the same ideologically driven policy-makers who seemed truly to believe, against all evidence, that invading US troops would be welcomed in the streets of Iraq with sweets and flowers. But their claimed focus on human rights and democracy did not find much currency early on; other powerful Washington political operatives understood that the American people were unlikely to embrace a large-scale and indefinite deployment of US troops to defend abstract visions of democracy or human rights. So for most top Bush officials, those high-minded goals took the pride of place only later on, when their originally chosen rationales were beginning to crumble, lie after lie. Eventually even credulous Americans (at least most of them) came to recognize the lies that underlay administration claims of WMDs, nuclear weapons programs, uranium yellowcake in Niger, Iraqi links to al-Qaeda, and Iraqi involvement in September 11—and only then did the issue of democracy move to center stage as an excuse for war.

The first explicit claims that democracy was the primary rationale for war in Iraq came in a speech by President George W. Bush on November 6, 2003, made as the public was becoming more aware of the lies regarding weapons of mass destruction. The speech called for a "forward strategy of freedom," linking his claimed commitment to democratization in Iraq and elsewhere in the Middle East to Ronald Reagan's Cold War call for democratization in Eastern Europe.

Much of the "democracy" framework that Bush tried to assert about Iraq had to do with the electoral process imposed by the US occupation forces. Certainly elections are often important as both indices and instruments of democracy, but elections held under conditions of military occupation can never be fully legitimate. President Bush had one thing right when he said in March 2005, "All [foreign] military forces and intelligence personnel must withdraw before the… elections for those elections to be free and fair."[15] Unfortunately, however, he was talking about Syrian troops in Lebanon; he made no mention of a parallel need for foreign forces to withdraw from Iraq to make *those* elections free and fair. The initial plan for elections in Iraq was designed to provide a veneer of credibility and legitimacy to the continuation of US control of the country. The strategy was to draft a US-oriented constitution and elect a US-friendly government that would welcome permanent US military bases in Iraq and maintain the US-imposed privatization and corporate-friendly economic regulations—in other words, to elect a government that would welcome continued US occupation under another name. As the Project on Defense Alternatives noted, the US goals in Iraq aimed

> to virtually reinvent the nation—economically, socially, and politically. The mission also has aimed to *substantially decide the future political balance inside Iraq* and to establish the country as a reliable ally and base for US operations. In the Administration's vision, Iraq is meant to serve not only as an example, but also as a "lever arm" for a program of coercive transformation throughout the region, affecting both the external behavior and internal constitution of Arab and Muslim states. [emphasis added]

Implementation of those goals led to the firing of the Iraqi military and police forces as well as virtually the entire civil service, privileging of US-backed Iraqi expatriates, creation of "elected" bodies delegitimized by their association with the US, and more.[16]

So implementation of the "democratization" strategy involved, from the beginning, powerful US political operations in Iraq designed to control the outcome of the series of elections. Despite official denials, it was quite clear that American financial and political influence-buying was extensive. Both the National Democratic Institute (NDI) and the International Republican Institute (IRI) launched major campaigns to help "train" and provide "capacity building" to various Iraqi political parties. These services were ostensibly available to all parties, but they certainly favored those deemed most open to maintaining close ties with the US occupation authorities and those viewed as likely to liberalize Iraq's economy—especially its central oil industry— and move it toward privatization and integration into the global market. The US Agency for International Development provided about $80 million to NDI, IRI, and other similar organizations, many of them working under the auspices of the Cold War–era National Endowment for Democracy, to "assist" Iraqi parties in the run-up to the elections.

The election processes caused serious escalation of the growing sectarian divides within Iraq. In a country whose social fabric had been brutally shredded by a dozen years of economic sanctions, continued bombings, invasion, and military occupation, the tendency to retreat from Iraq's traditional secular national identity increased, leading to smaller associations and alliances based on religion, ethnicity, tribe, clan, and family. The US supported the creation of a new set of political parties based largely on ethnic and/or religious identity, which continued the fragmentation of Iraqi national identity. Washington's early embrace of Kurdish and Shi'a-based parties (which happened to be based in Iraq's oil-richest zones), combined with its efforts to win the appearance of legitimacy and to undercut the resistance by convincing Sunni politicians to join the electoral process, continued this process of the devolution of Iraqi national identity and national power to smaller religious and ethnic sub-groups.

As sectarian violence rose in early 2006, and especially as White House threats to expand the war to Iran increased, the US shifted some of its political support, particularly distancing itself from some of the key pro-Iranian Shi'a parties. More than six months after the January 2006 election of a "permanent" Iraqi government, fractious parliamen-tarians remained unable to choose a cabinet. From the beginning of the occupation, US efforts to "bring democracy" had the effect of dividing Iraq and Iraqis by ethnic and religious affiliations and so undercutting Iraqi national identity.

Following the 2003 invasion, the US began the process of imposing "democracy" on Iraq in June 2004. US proconsul Paul Bremer left Baghdad and "transferred sovereignty" from the officially US-run Coalition Provisional Authority to an "interim government" of US-chosen Iraqi officials. But Bremer's version of "sovereignty" kept in place 140,000 US troops, 20,000 non-US "coalition" troops, and tens of thousands of private military contractors still occupying Iraq. He had imposed 97 new laws and regulations, which the US occupation authorities themselves identified as "binding instructions or directives to the Iraqi people." He had appointed a powerful electoral commission with authority to disqualify any parties or candidates it chose, as well as approving national security and intelligence chiefs for Iraq, each of whom was promised a five-year term. Bremer himself, referring to the complex web of regulations, acknowledged they were put in place to impose permanent changes in Iraq, noting that "you set up these things... and it's harder to reverse course."[17]

Following what the US called the "transition to sovereignty," Iraq's economy remained dependent on and reflective of US priorities. Bremer's economic regulations included capping taxes at 15 percent, guaranteeing the right to allow up to 100 percent foreign ownership of all Iraqi entities, corporate regulations designed to qualify Iraq for the WTO, and continued protection for companies (such as Halliburton) with oil-related contracts signed before the hand-over. According to Mahmoud Othman, a Kurdish member of the earlier US-appointed

Governing Council, the US authorities "have established a system to meddle in our affairs."[18] As author Naomi Klein noted just months after the US invasion, "on September 19, [2003], Bremer enacted the now-infamous Order 39. It announced that 200 Iraqi state companies would be privatized; decreed that foreign firms can retain 100 percent ownership of Iraqi banks, mines and factories; and allowed these firms to move 100 percent of their profits out of Iraq. *The Economist* declared the new rules a 'capitalist dream.'"[19] But it was not only a capitalist dream; it also put the "new" Iraq completely outside the traditions of every Arab country in the region. No other country, oil-producing or not, allowed this level of privatization; no country (virtually anywhere in the world!) allowed 100 percent foreign ownership of national resources. This was the fastest, most radical economic restructuring effort the world had ever seen.

This meddling then moved toward elections that would ostensibly represent real democracy for Iraqis in choosing their own government. Certainly Iraqis were eager for real democracy and eager to choose their own leaders, and the millions who poured into the streets to vote in January 2005 in defiance of serious threats from a variety of sectarian and other forces showed extraordinary courage. But the elections, and the limited, derivative power given to the new government, would all take place under and be limited by the reality of continuing war and military occupation. Iraq was not sovereign, and holding elections did not make it so. Iraq's continuing violence prevented most credible international election monitors from even observing the elections; the UN sent only 35 staffers, and the high-profile International Mission for Iraqi Elections announced they would monitor the elections from outside Iraq, in neighboring Jordan. The Carter Center said they could not send observers at all because of the lack of security; such a judgment would almost inevitably result in elections that could not be deemed free, fair, or democratic. Similar weaknesses undermined the October 2005 vote on an Iraqi constitution—a text drafted largely by US lawyers contracted to the State Department.

In response to a global outcry against the election process being orchestrated by the US in Iraq, the once-defiant but now submissive United Nations moved to defend the US occupation. UN experts asserted that there was in fact a precedent for "legitimate" elections held under military occupation. Their model of choice was the 1999 UN-run election in East Timor. But they ignored the significant differences. Since 1976, UN resolutions had officially deemed the 1975 Indonesian occupation illegal and called on Jakarta to withdraw from East Timor. The 1999 vote was not to select a puppet "government" to administer East Timor under continuing Indonesian occupation as was the case later in Iraq, but instead was a direct referendum on whether or not to end the occupation—a choice never offered to Iraqis.

Additionally, the Indonesian military was under sufficient pressure that there was little military violence during the referendum itself. (The Indonesian military's razing of much of the East Timorese capital of Dili came after the election.)

In fact, despite US control of the process, most of the parties chosen in the Iraqi elections came into power having promised that their first act would be to request that US troops leave Iraq. But it should be no surprise that the elected parliamentarians of those same parties, once they took office under the protection of US occupation troops in the US-controlled "Green Zone," quickly abandoned their campaign promises. By 2007, however, a majority of Iraqi parliamentarians reclaimed their opposition to the occupation, and began to pass resolutions and issue letters demanding that the US-backed "sovereign" government of Prime Minister Nuri al-Maliki follow suit and impose a timetable for the withdrawal of occupation troops. Recognizing that he would have no chance of remaining in power without US backing, Maliki refused, and a long stalemate between the US-backed government and the parliament ensued.

What war crimes have been committed in Iraq?

War crimes are violations of the international laws governing warfare. War crimes include such acts as deliberately targeting civilians, attacking military targets when the effect is disproportionately harmful to civilians, or violating the Fourth Geneva Convention's requirements for humane treatment of civilians, wounded combatants, or prisoners of war in wartime. The US has a long history of war crimes in Iraq that predates the current war and occupation. During the 1991 Operation Desert Storm in Iraq, the US committed numerous war crimes, including bombing a civilian air raid shelter and killing more than 400 civilians sheltering there and attacking Iraqi troops fleeing Kuwait as they tried to surrender. The Pentagon's specific intention to destroy Iraq's electrical facilities despite the life-threatening consequences for civilian life-support systems such as water treatment also qualifies those bombings as war crimes.[20] In all those instances, President George H.W. Bush and his top military and civilian advisors should have faced trial for war crimes in a US or international court.

The twelve years of economic sanctions that followed, which resulted in the deaths of more than 500,000 Iraqi children, were also an enormous war crime. Then Secretary of State Madeleine Albright's infamous statement regarding those children—"we think the price is worth it"[21]—did not make such violations legal.

The US invasion of Iraq began as what the Nuremberg principles identify as the worst war crime: a crime against peace in the form of a war of aggression. Then UN Secretary-General Kofi Annan stated that "from the [UN] Charter point of view, it was illegal."[22] The Jury of Conscience of the World Tribunal on Iraq, meeting in Istanbul in June 2005, found the governments of the US and the UK guilty of "planning, preparing, and waging the supreme crime of a war of aggression in contravention of the United Nations Charter and the Nuremberg Principles."[23] The violation was particularly egregious since the extensive prewar claims made by the Bush administration and by British Prime Minister Tony Blair regarding the "imminent" threat posed by Iraq's alleged stockpiles of weapons of mass destruction turned out to be false.

Once the war began, the March 2003 "shock and awe" campaign, designed specifically to terrorize Iraqi civilians, violated the Geneva Convention's prohibitions against targeting civilians and attacking military targets with disproportionate harm to civilians. Those prohibitions include "violence to life and person, in particular murder of all kinds, mutilation, cruel treatment and torture… The passing of sentences and the carrying out of executions without previous judgment pronounced by a regularly constituted court affording all the judicial guarantees which are recognized as indispensable by civilized peoples."[24] It is in the context of this wide-ranging set of deliberate war crimes—enabled by policy decisions at the very highest levels of US political and military leaders—that the specific illegal acts by US soldiers in Abu Ghraib, in Haditha, Fallujah, and elsewhere across Iraq, which have become common knowledge throughout the world, took place.

The leveling of Fallujah in 2004 was a war crime; much of the civilian population remains displaced from their homes almost four years later. The UN's High Commissioner for Human Rights, Louise Arbour, denounced the killings of civilians and injured people in Fallujah and registered a complaint regarding the lack of access to civilians by independent international humanitarian aid workers. "All violations of international humanitarian law and human rights law must be investigated and those responsible for breaches—including the deliberate targeting of civilians, indiscriminate and disproportionate attacks, the killing of injured persons and the use of human shields—must be brought to justice, be they members of the multinational force or insurgents," she said.[25] In the context of international and especially United Nations–style diplomacy, asserting the equivalence of the US occupation forces and the Iraqi resistance represented a major political accomplishment.

There is no question that some resistance forces in Iraq have committed war crimes as well. All attacks on civilians, whether part of the sectarian ethnic cleansing that the US-led occupation enabled, or attacks designed to intimidate real or alleged collaborators by targeting their families, are violations of the laws of war for resistance fighters as well as occupation forces.

In an innovative effort to broaden the definition of "war crimes," a witness to the 2005 World Tribunal on Iraq testified that "the will of the global antiwar movement, a will that has been clearly and repeatedly made manifest through demonstrations, declarations, petitions, statements, and acts, has been knowingly and purposely violated by the government of the United States and its allies through the perpetration of the war on Iraq and the continuing occupation." He called on the Tribunal's jury "to recognize this violation as a blatant crime against peace."[26]

Do Iraqis have the right to resist?

According to international law, a population subject to an "alien occupation" has the right to resist "in exercise of their right of self-determination, as enshrined in the Charter of the United Nations."[27] The forms of resistance can vary widely, from cultural mobilization and anti-occupation education and advocacy to nonviolent protest marches to legal challenges in national or international courts. Legal resistance can also include the use of military force to resist a foreign military occupation. The right of armed resistance is not absolute (i.e., attacking civilians is always prohibited), but attacking the occupying army is legal. For the occupying troops, on the other hand, almost any military action aimed at the indigenous civilian population in the country they are occupying will be illegal.

Despite the challenges of surviving a violent military occupation and a host of often brutal internal conflicts, Iraqis continue mobilizing to support civil, social, economic, and political life, including work to obtain access to the basic human necessities (food, water, health care, education, etc.) that the US–UK occupation fails to provide. The Iraqi oil workers' unions, which have built strong ties with US Labor Against the War and counterpart organizations in Britain, are one of the examples most familiar to US–UK antiwar campaigners. A panoply of other organizations fighting for women's rights, legal and civil rights, access to education, and a host of other causes also function, always under harsh conditions.

Some groups attempt to mobilize direct nonviolent resistance to the occupation, a strategic task incredibly difficult under conditions of such unrelenting war and violence. Little more than a year after the invasion of Iraq, the *Christian Science Monitor* described how

> In one of Baghdad's fiercest hotbeds of anti-American violence, something different is happening: Two weeks ago, young men and old walked down the street holding up banners protesting US military incursions. They used their mouths, not their guns. ... [I]n January a dozen residents—a group of childhood friends—decided that people needed a voice for their political views and formed a nonviolent political group. While some residents remain skeptical—some are unsure of the direction it will take, others say that Americans will only listen to force—many

hope this is the seed of a new movement. "We want to be assured the resistance will respect democracy, rights of women, different religions. We don't want types like Al Qaeda… and Saddam," says Wahdi Nadhmi, a political analyst and professor at Baghdad University. "If the patriotic elements start a civil struggle, it will be welcomed by most Iraqi people."[28]

While such mobilizations struggle against extraordinary odds, they have survived. Beginning in 2006 the Iraqi Nonviolence Group, known as LAONF for the Arabic word for nonviolence, has linked more than 100 local civil society groups across the country. LAONF defines itself as

> organisations and individuals with different ideological and political background, gathering around the idea of non-violence as the most effective way to struggle for an independent, democratic, peaceful Iraq…. This group believes in a humanitarian approach to non-violent struggle, which is made real through supporting any non-violence movement and group of activists all around the world. We refuse occupation and war as a way to build democracy and establish rule of law, even when it is presented as the only possible option: we believe in promoting peace culture and dialogue instead.[29]

Other organizations work on specific issues; for instance, the Justice Network for Prisoners monitors conditions in prisons run by the Iraqi government and military.[30] All these organizations are backed by international antiwar campaigners and networks.

But little of this activity reaches the mainstream media. So it is perhaps not surprising that as a whole, the term "the Iraqi resistance" is usually used to refer to the range of military organizations, some of them militias tied to political parties, others made up of former Iraqi military forces, others that operate independently as clandestine cells.

Certainly some of the resistance is made up of ordinary Iraqis, religious and secular, such as those powerfully documented in the excellent 2007 film *Meeting Resistance*, who took to armed opposition—as is their legal right—as a means of ridding their country of an illegal occupation. But—other than the Mahdi Army of Moqtada al-Sadr, the most powerful and prominent resistance group until its 2007 ceasefire—the most identifiable and certainly most powerful components of the armed resistance appear to be a diverse set of largely unconnected and often antagonistic armed movements, some of which, such as the terrorist organization known as al-Qaeda in Iraq, attack Iraqi civilians as much or even more than they do occupation troops. The most influential groups are based in specific religious or ethnic communities, and while secular armed forces certainly exist, it is the various religious resistance movements that have taken pride of place in occupied Iraq. Little is known of what most of the factions stand for beyond their opposition to the US occupation; what is most frequently made public are highly sectarian agendas. There is no unified national resistance program defining exactly what the fight is against or for. And unlike in other anti-occupation, anti-colonial, and national resistance movements, there is no unified leadership that can speak for "the resistance" as a whole.

As a result, while antiwar and anti-occupation views are dominant around the world, there is little international support for the actual organizations carrying out the armed resistance in Iraq. The situation does not match the global solidarity movements that made support for the National Liberation Front (NLF, or "Viet Cong") in Vietnam, or the African National Congress in apartheid South Africa, or the Sandinista Front and FMLN in Central America, central to their broader antiwar, anti-apartheid, or anti-intervention work.

Those liberation movements had a legitimate claim to real national leadership and international influence partly because they held themselves accountable to their population as a whole, but equally because global campaigners understood and supported their overall social program. We may not have agreed with every position or every tactic, but overall we shared not only what they were fighting *against*—US-backed dictatorships or US-paid Contra guerrillas or the devastation of apartheid—but what they were fighting *for* as well: independence and socialism in

Vietnam, self-determination and social justice in Central America, a non-racial South Africa.

That isn't the case in Iraq. Building a powerful global movement to end the US–UK occupation of Iraq requires real internationalism. This means making good on US and UK activists' obligations to end the war and occupation, and recognizing the Iraqis' right to resist. But internationalism does not require embracing any particular armed resistance organizations or forces that happen to be in motion today, especially if they routinely target civilians, or seek implementation of extremist religious laws anywhere they may obtain influence.

—PART II—

THE US AT WAR

Doesn't the Iraq war make us safer against another terrorist attack like 9/11? Shouldn't we "fight them there so we don't have to fight them here"?

Iraq was not responsible for the attacks of September 11, 2001. Saddam Hussein and his government had no ties to al-Qaeda and there were no al-Qaeda operatives in Iraq; in fact there was enormous hostility between the ruthlessly secular Iraqi government and the Islamist extremists of al-Qaeda. (When Iraq invaded Kuwait in 1990, and the US announced plans to send troops to Saudi Arabia en route to Kuwait, Osama bin Laden offered to send 100,000 "Islamic warriors" to defend Saudi Arabia from the "infidels.") Instead of making the US safer, global opposition to the US invasion and occupation of Iraq has grown and sharpened, and many people in other countries no longer distinguish between US policy and the American people. In Arab and Muslim countries, where opposition is most powerful, that antagonism sometimes takes a military or violent form. The result is that Americans around the world are less safe as a result of the war in Iraq.

The notion that "we have to fight them there so we don't have to fight them here" is based on several false claims. The notion of "them" is rooted not in a clear assessment of a particular government or even organization, but rather in a fundamentally racist view of "them" as the ultimate "other." "They" are Muslim; "they" are Arab or Persian; "they" are not like "us"—

because "we" are democratic, western, secular (even if Christian or Jewish), and—sotto voce—white.

There were no foreign terrorists in Iraq before the US invasion. Iraq's repressive regime carried out massive human rights violations against its own people, but the export of terrorism was not part of its methodology. Its borders were secure and international terrorists knew they would find no safety in Iraq. (The one exception was in the US-protected Kurdish enclave in northern Iraq, which was not under the Baghdad government's control from 1991 on. A small organization apparently allied with al-Qaeda found refuge in that US- and British-protected "no-fly zone.") In the State Department's 2001 edition of its annual *Patterns of Global Terrorism*, the US acknowledged that Iraq "has not attempted an anti-Western attack since its failed plot to assassinate former President Bush in 1993 in Kuwait." (In fact questions remain as to whether that alleged assassination attempt even happened, and if it did, whether there was Iraqi involvement.)

But the US invasion has changed all that. Iraq's border guards were demobilized, making its once-impermeable borders porous. Iraq has been transformed into a gathering place for not only anti-occupation or even anti-US fighters, but for global terrorists with extremist and sectarian agendas, willing to kill civilians as much as occupation troops. So the US invasion and occupation have endangered Iraqis and others in the region as well as Americans.

What are the human, economic, and other costs to the US?

In the spring of 2008, when US military deaths in Iraq hit the milestone 4,000 mark, many were stunned. A poll weeks earlier had indicated extraordinarily low level of media coverage of the war—an average of only 15 percent of news stories and airtime for most of 2007, but a shockingly reduced 1–3 percent by January–February 2008.[31] The overall lack of press attention reflected the success of a multifaceted effort by the Bush administration to suppress public awareness of the costs and consequences of the war.

One part of that strategy included such methods as prohibiting the longstanding tradition of filming the return of the flag-draped coffins of dead soldiers and limiting private administration officials' meetings with soldiers' families and wounded soldiers. The 4,000 dead soldiers were appropriately identified, and with some effort journalists and others could find the details of how they died. But parallel information regarding the wounded remains much more difficult. Pentagon and administration figures of 26,000 to 30,000 wounded troops include only limited categories: only those wounded by hostile fire in officially designated combat are included, meaning those injured badly enough in training exercises to require amputation, or gravely injured in helicopter accidents, let alone disabilities from diseases they would not have gotten if they were not in Iraq, are not included. Only injuries serious enough to require transit out of Iraq are included; those treated in country are not. And crucially, mental health issues are not included at all, so the huge numbers of troops coming back from Iraq with PTSD (post-traumatic stress disorder) are not included in any count. Those number from about 17 percent of those who have served in Iraq, according to the *New England Journal of Medicine* in a study conducted in the first year of the war,[32] to as much as 30 percent, according to Dr. Arthur Blank, a psychiatrist and the leading American expert in treating PTSD, testifying in a court hearing just days before the fifth anniversary of the US invasion.[33]

In its efforts to promote the war as successful and hide its true human and financial costs, the Bush administration is also involved in much more overt media management and direct propaganda. In a bombshell front-page exposé in the *New York Times*, a group of over 75 retired military officers familiar to television, radio, and other media consumers as "military analysts" examining developments in the Iraq war were exposed as the centerpiece of

> a Pentagon information apparatus that has used those analysts in a campaign to generate favorable news coverage of the administration's wartime performance. ... The effort, which began with the buildup to the Iraq war and continues to this day, has sought to exploit ideological and military allegiances, and also a powerful financial dynamic: Most of the

analysts have ties to military contractors vested
in the very war policies they are asked to assess
on air.[34]

The comprehensive article went on to identify how
the admirals and generals, chosen for their appearance
of expertise and objectivity, were given private
briefings by high-ranking administration officials
including Vice President Cheney, then Attorney
General Alberto Gonzales, National Security Advisor
Stephen Hadley, and others; private tours of Iraq and
the Guantánamo Bay prison; access to classified
intelligence inaccessible to others, and more. The
propaganda campaign allowed the defense companies
the analysts worked for to brag about their private
sources of information, the key currency in the highly
competitive effort to win Pentagon contracts. It also
provided the administration itself with spokespeople
parroting the White House line of the day to the
American people from within the television and radio
studios as if reflecting an independent judgment. In
fact, as the *Times* investigation revealed,

> members of this group have echoed admini-
> stration talking points, sometimes even when
> they suspected the information was false or
> inflated. Some analysts acknowledge they
> suppressed doubts because they feared
> jeopardizing their access. ... Kenneth Allard, a
> former NBC military analyst who has taught
> information warfare at the National Defense
> University, said the campaign amounted to a

sophisticated information operation. ... As conditions in Iraq deteriorated, Mr. Allard recalled, he saw a yawning gap between what analysts were told in private briefings and what subsequent inquiries and books later revealed. "Night and day," Mr. Allard said, "I felt we'd been hosed."

The military analysts served, the *Times* concluded, as "a kind of media Trojan horse—an instrument intended to shape terrorism coverage from inside the major TV and radio networks." It was an extraordinarily brazen strategy, of which then Secretary of Defense Donald Rumsfeld was the author.

The Bush administration's strategy of hiding the war's consequences also extended to preventing public awareness of the financial and social costs of the war. As the 2007–2008 economic crisis escalated in the US, little of the rising concern reflected the role of the Iraq war—as well as the war in Afghanistan and the broader "global war on terror"—in impoverishing the United States. When Nobel economic laureate Joseph Stiglitz and his Harvard colleague Linda Bilmes published their book *The Three Trillion Dollar War*, the response was also disbelief. But only because the real costs had been disguised and distorted from the beginning. When Bush's chief economic advisor, Lawrence Lindsay, estimated that war in Iraq might cost as much as $100 to $200 billion, Secretary of Defense Donald Rumsfeld called his statement "baloney." Then Lindsay was fired. In fact, by the spring of 2008, war spending had passed $526 billion,[35] another $200 billion was already in the pipeline, and paying just for existing future commitments would bring the total to $1.5 trillion.

As of March 2008, the breakdown was as follows:

Iraq spending to date: **$526 billion**
Future military operations (through 2017):
    $669 billion
Veterans costs (medical, disability, social security):
    $630 billion
Social costs (veterans' medical care, anticipated losses from deaths & injury): **$367 billion**
Interest (paid to date, plus future interest on current & future borrowing): **$616 billion**[36]

The additional costs to families and communities are enormous as well. The high rate of survival of young soldiers with devastating multiple injuries means that the families of tens of thousands of returning troops are now facing the human, social, physical, and financial challenges of arranging care, sometimes 24/7 nursing care, for recently healthy but now completely disabled people who may require that care for another 50 years. Despite some budget increases, huge shortfalls in staff and facilities continue to plague both the Veterans Administration and active-duty military medical systems. As a result, and particularly because so many of the troops, and thus so many of the injured, are from rural areas and small towns, the necessary facilities are often not accessible, meaning additional sacrifices, abandoned careers, divided families, and more. (The impact— economic, social and otherwise—of US-based private military contractors killed or returning home with grievous combat injuries remains untallied. Privatization mavens at the Pentagon claimed from the beginning that despite their sky-high salaries, the fact that the US military [read: taxpayers] would not be responsible for medical care for corporate-hired security contractors was one more reason that out-sourcing the war would be economical. But when their limited private insurance runs out, it will ultimately mean that medical and other costs, perhaps lifetime care costs, will be turned over to community and/or state sources. So taxpayers will pay anyway.)

Almost one-third of the US troops now in Iraq are from the National Guard and Reserve. Those multiple deployments have taken a huge toll on the "first responders" in many communities—paramedics, firefighters, ambulance drivers, and others on the front line of emergency response work, and who are disproportionately represented in the Guard and Reserve. The impact of the Iraq war on the 2005 Katrina disaster was a clear example: it was apparent to everyone watching that the response to Katrina was significantly weakened because so few members of the National Guard were available—so many of them, and so much of their crucial equipment, were in Iraq.

Finally, the war has exacted great cost to the US's already damaged democracy. The fact that almost 70 percent of the US population want the war to end immediately or very soon, and that almost two-thirds believe it was never worth fighting in the first place, is deemed irrelevant by Bush administration officials, Congress, and the media. When asked about the large majorities of Americans who oppose the war, Vice President Cheney answered simply and memorably: "So?" Members of Congress elected on pledges to end the war instead complain that they don't have the votes necessary to override a presidential veto— ignoring the fact that no veto would be necessary if the Democratic majority simply refused to vote each supplemental war spending bill out of committee in the first place. The mainstream media engaged in a modicum of *mea culpa*s for their pre- and early-war cheerleading for administration lies on Iraq's WMDs, links to 9/11, and other claims, but soon fell into the same patterns with largely uncritical backing of the "surge" and an uncritical acceptance of the White House's campaign to demonize Iran. The increasing cynicism among young people about their government's lack of responsiveness and the sense of helplessness and often hopelessness among so many Americans bodes dangerously ill.

Why did the US and UK invade Iraq?
The pretexts for the US–UK invasion are well known: weapons of mass destruction, links with al-Qaeda,

nuclear mushroom clouds. They were asserted over and over again.

In a carefully orchestrated media campaign the fall 2001 anthrax attacks in the US were also—and equally falsely—blamed on Iraq. During that period, 2008 Republican presidential candidate John McCain said directly that "some of this anthrax may—and I emphasize may—have come from Iraq." (In the summer of 2008, when the FBI's unproven but ostensible "lead suspect" in the anthrax attacks committed suicide before being indicted, it was particularly ironic to note that the only thing actually known about the attacks was that the anthrax did not come from abroad, but from a US government laboratory. And the only thing linking anthrax to Iraq was the fact that during the 1980s, when the US alliance with Saddam Hussein in Iraq was strong, a US company, the American Type Culture Collection, was licensed by the US Commerce Department to provide anthrax germs, among other biological agents, directly to the Iraqi government.)

As we know, all of these pretexts proved to be false. New evidence of the falsehoods continues to surface. As recently as August 2008, Ron Suskind's explosive book *The Way of the World* documented for the first time how the CIA, at the request of the White House, forged a letter supposedly written to Saddam Hussein by his intelligence director. Backdated to July 1, 2001, before the September 11 attacks, it was released months into the 2003 invasion just as US claims regarding WMD, nuclear weapons, and Iraqi links to terrorism were all collapsing. The letter—over the signature of Iraq's intelligence director, who had already told the US that Iraq had no WMDs and had then been paid $5 million hush money—covered the rest of the Bush administration's favorite pretext: It stated that 9/11 leader Mohamed Atta trained for the attack in Iraq, a claim that, if true, would have proved the Iraq–al-Qaeda link. Except that the entire letter was a forgery, made possible because British intelligence had recruited Saddam Hussein's intelligence chief in the run-up to the US–UK invasion. It was all a lie.

So what were the real reasons? For the US, they come down to oil, power, and ideology. All three are inextricably linked. For the UK, those three reasons took a back seat to the fundamental political goal of maintaining the "special" Bush–Blair partnership within the broader US–UK alliance, with London eager to prove itself Washington's indispensable partner.

Economic and strategic powerbrokers have coveted Iraqi oil—the second- or third-largest reserves in the world—for over a century, starting with the British in the early twentieth century and continuing to the US today. US concern today is not about immediate access—the global oil market is quite fungible and once any country's oil is on the market it is available for all comers; also, the US in recent years has significantly decreased its import of Middle Eastern oil in favor of oil from Canada, Mexico, Venezuela, Angola, Nigeria, and other sources. The real concern was and remains that of control. Whoever controls Iraq's vast oil fields, as is true for Iran, Saudi Arabia, and other key sources, controls pricing, production quotas, decisions regarding which international oil companies will gain or lose contracts, and more. If the US can be the guarantor of access to Iraq's oil resources, it automatically wields enormous power over its allies (such as Germany and Japan, who are both far more reliant on Middle Eastern oil than the US). It also holds sway over its competitors and challengers, such as China, with the power to grant privileged access to one group of oil companies, while denying any access at all to other oil firms. (See also "What does oil have to do with the Iraq war?")

If the US could completely control Iraq and its oil industry, it would have a new center from which to project US military might at the very heart of the oil-rich and strategically situated Middle East. Iraq would become a giant military base—within which the fifteen-plus mega-bases built by the Pentagon in the years of the US occupation, as well as the scores of smaller bases, would play starring roles. Iraq would become a jumping off point for military interventions in hotspots elsewhere in the region.

Occupied Iraq would have provided all that—were it not for the inconvenient fact that the Iraqi people resisted occupation, a resistance that under the strain of occupation has also created civil war.

For Bush, Cheney, and the neoconservative cabal that shaped the call for war in Iraq long before 9/11, the real reason was ideology. These ideologues appear to actually believe that the nations and peoples of the Middle East were—and perhaps still are—just waiting for US troops and tanks to invade their countries, destroy their governments, dismantle their armies and police, shred their civil society, impoverish their people, and take over their economy. They would welcome the troops with sweets and flowers and singing in the streets. And they would call it democracy. It is an old illusion long held by occupiers of others' lands—first described more than 2,000 years ago by the great war correspondent Tacitus, who followed the Roman legions as they laid waste to the far reaches of the empire. "The Romans brought devastation," Tacitus wrote after one particularly brutal battle, "but they called it peace."

When the Bush administration linked that ideological framework to an unshakeable strategic commitment to militarism and unilateralism, and took advantage of the post-9/11 fear that immobilized so much of American civil life and political institutions, including Congress, its drive toward war became unstoppable.

What kind of relationship did the US have with Iraq before the 2003 invasion, war, and occupation?

The US has had a longstanding relationship with Iraq

dating back to the 1920s, when it joined Britain, then the League of Nations Mandatory power in Iraq, in a consortium to exploit Iraqi oil. More recently, following the 1958 revolution in Iraq that overthrew the British-backed monarchy, Iraq's leaders cultivated close ties with the US. In fact, the CIA helped orchestrate the coup within the Ba'ath Party that brought Saddam Hussein's faction to power in 1968, and the US backed him when he seized full power as president in 1979. When Iraq invaded Iran in 1980, the US provided arms to both sides, hoping to maximize the loss of lives and economic cost to both countries, either of which could become a potential challenger to US regional hegemony. But the US actively favored Iraq, which it deemed the weaker of the two, and provided Saddam Hussein's government with satellite targeting information for more precise use of chemical weapons, conventional arms and loan guarantees, and seed stock for biological weapons.

The US maintained a close alliance with Iraq all through the 1980s. In 1983, and again in 1984, Donald Rumsfeld, then the special envoy of President Reagan, traveled to Baghdad to meet with Saddam Hussein and negotiate a renewal of full US–Iraqi diplomatic relations, which many of Rumsfeld's backers hoped would lead to oil deals as well. Despite at least two face-to-face meetings, Rumsfeld never expressed to Saddam Hussein any US government displeasure about Iraq's use of illegal chemical weapons against Iranian troops or Kurdish civilians.

(The State Department claims without evidence that Rumsfeld did mention it separately to Tariq Aziz, Iraq's foreign minister.) In any case, Washington restored full diplomatic relations by November 1984, extending financial support, agricultural credits, military technology and intelligence, and more.

It was during its alliance with the United States in the 1970s and 1980s that Iraq began its programs aimed toward producing chemical and biological weapons and its research into nuclear weapons. These programs were actively supported by US corporations as well as the US government, as revealed in 1994 Senate Banking Committee hearings. According to Senator Donald W. Riegle, chairman of the committee:

> We do know that the United States licensed the export of genetic materials capable of being used to create these types of genetically-altered biological warfare agents to the Iraqi Atomic Energy Commission—an Iraqi governmental agency that conducted biological warfare-related research—prior to the war. One method of creating these genetically altered micro-organisms is by exposing them to radiation. The United States also licensed that export of several species of brucella to Iraqi governmental agencies. Both Q-fever and brucellosis are also endemic to the region.[38]

Further verification emerged later in a leak to the German newspaper *Die Tageszeitung* of some of the

8,000 pages that Washington had secretly excised from Iraq's December 7, 2002 UN arms declaration before allowing other members of the Security Council to see the material. The deleted sections documented the role of 24 US corporations, 55 US subsidiaries of foreign corporations, and a number of US government agencies in providing parts, material, training, and other assistance to Iraq's chemical, biological, missile, and nuclear weapons programs throughout the 1970s and 1980s, some continuing till the end of 1990. The US corporations included Honeywell, Rockwell, Hewlett Packard, Dupont, Eastman Kodak, and Bechtel. US government agencies, including the Departments of Energy, Commerce, Defense, and Agriculture, as well as federal laboratories at Sandia, Los Alamos and Lawrence Livermore, were also involved in assisting or provisioning Iraq's military—including WMD—capacity.[39]

Not only Rumsfeld but other Republican insiders were involved in shady deals that helped build Iraq's WMDs. In 1989, news broke of a secret $4 billion loan made to Iraq by a US branch of Banca Nazionale del Lavoro (BNL) of Italy, which at the time employed Henry Kissinger on its Consulting Board for International Policy. Congressman Henry Gonzalez, chair of the House Banking Committee, also noted that an executive of Kissinger Associates met Saddam Hussein in Baghdad in June 1989 at a meeting in which the Iraqi leader apparently expressed interest in expanding commercial relations with the US. "Many

Kissinger Associates clients received US export licenses for exports to Iraq. Several were also the beneficiaries of BNL loans to Iraq," Congressman Gonzalez wrote in a letter to then President George H.W. Bush. Iraq also used the BNL loans to attempt to buy difficult-to-manufacture nuclear weapons components.[40]

In July 1990, only days before Iraq invaded Kuwait, US Ambassador April Glaspie met with Saddam Hussein and told him, on behalf of President George H.W. Bush, that "we have no opinion on the Arab–Arab conflicts, like your border disagreement with Kuwait."[41] Some analysts believe Saddam Hussein interpreted this as a green light for Iraq to invade Kuwait. Whether or not this was the case, it clearly was *not* an unequivocal statement that the US opposed such an invasion.

Washington's position toward its former ally Saddam Hussein and his Ba'athist regime changed abruptly after Iraq invaded Kuwait in August 1990. The invasion, itself a clear violation of international law, provided the US with a convenient pretext for an unnecessary war. The war mobilization of 1990–1991 reflected a policy choice, not a policy necessity. Iraq was not, after all, the first Middle Eastern country to invade and occupy a neighbor. Morocco remained occupying Western Sahara; Turkey had invaded Northern Cyprus and maintained a rump "Turkish Republic" there since 1974; and Israel continued its internationally condemned occupation of the Palestinian West Bank, Gaza, and East Jerusalem, as well as the Syrian Golan Heights. All those occupations were illegal, and like Iraq's invasion of Kuwait, were carried out by close allies of the US.

But in 1990 Washington was responding to something beyond Iraq and Kuwait: the broader international situation and the end of the Cold War. The Soviet Union was about to collapse, leaving the US as the sole global superpower. Instead of announcing a peace dividend and a pullback from its global military trajectory, the US decided to lead the world to war as a way of trumpeting its decision to remain a super-power, despite the lack of a strategic challenger. The alliance with Iraq was reversed, and the demonization of Saddam Hussein and all things Iraqi began. The first US war against Iraq, in 1991, the twelve years of crippling economic sanctions that Washington imposed in the name of the United Nations, and finally the 2003 invasion and occupation all reflected that process of demonization and delegitimization.

Was the US–UK invasion of Iraq legal? Is the war legal now?

The US and the UK had no legal right to invade Iraq. The UN Charter, while vague about some things, is absolutely clear about the two conditions under which a military attack is legal. One is if the Security Council itself explicitly authorizes a military strike in a decision taken under Article 42 of Chapter VII of the Charter. That was the kind of resolution the US and the UK pressed so hard for in the run-up to the

2003 invasion—and exactly the kind of resolution that was rejected by the Security Council. Washington and London gave up their efforts to win that resolution—as the Associated Press reported it, "rattled by an outpouring of international antiwar sentiment"[42]—and withdrew their draft text in the midst of the global protests on February 15, 2003.

The second justification for war is self-defense. But self-defense is a narrowly defined right. Under Article 51 of the UN Charter, every country has the right of self-defense only "*if* an armed attack occurs." Iraq had not attacked the US and was not capable of doing so, so there was no valid claim of self-defense. The US claimed a new "right" of what officials referred to as "preemptive self-defense" to go to war against Iraq without any further authorization from the United Nations. But nothing in the UN Charter legitimizes such a claim. Some scholars believe that an effort to stop an imminent attack would also legalize a country's right to use military force in a preemptive kind of self-defense. But even that argument fails, because no one, even the Bush super-hawks, claimed that an Iraqi attack of any sort, especially on the United States, was "imminent."

Instead, what the US and UK did in March 2003 was launch a preventive war of aggression. Going to war against another country to prevent some speculative future development has no legitimacy anywhere in international law. According to the 1950 Nuremberg Principles, "planning, preparation, initiation or waging of a war of aggression" constitutes a crime against peace.[43]

In the US, various apologists for the Iraq war, in and outside the Bush administration, claimed that the congressional authorization passed in November 2002 granting Bush permission to go to war somehow made the invasion legal. But the decisions of a nation's parliament do not supercede international law; Article VI of the US Constitution states that international treaties constitute part of the supreme law of the land. A decision by Congress to give the president the authority to go to war, in violation of numerous treaties, did not and could not make the war legal.

In May 2003, when UN resistance to the US's war drive collapsed, the Security Council passed a resolution "recognizing" the US and the UK as the "occupying powers" in Iraq. That resolution did not, however, retroactively legalize the original invasion; it merely identified Washington and London as occupying powers with the relevant obligations imposed by the Geneva Conventions and other parts of international law. The US and the UK would therefore be responsible for providing the civilian population of occupied Iraq with all required for their lives: security, clean water, medical care, food, education, etc. Those obligations on an occupying power also prohibit attacks on civilians, interference with the existing economy, taking control of the occupied country's resources, and far more.

In waging war in Iraq, the Bush administration, backed by Tony Blair, sought to legitimize the notion of preventive war as the basis for its international relations. In addition to undermining the restrictions on war imposed by the United Nations Charter and the Nuremberg principles, the war set a dangerous precedent for other countries to act as military aggressors in the future, seizing any opportunity to respond militarily to claimed potential future threats, whether real or contrived, that must be "preventively" controlled. The Iraq war has set the stage for military anarchy and uncontrolled nationalist ambition and militarism on a global scale. Luckily, other countries have not seized on the war as a model for their own behavior. At least not yet.

Didn't the US troops in Iraq all volunteer to be there?

The US troops fighting in Iraq (and Afghanistan, Pakistan, Somalia, the Philippines, and elsewhere in the so-called global war on terror) were not forced to join the military through a legal draft as was the case during the Vietnam War. But there is no question that the majority of young men and women enlisting today are in fact subject to a draft: a draft in the form of poverty, lack of opportunities, unaffordable college tuitions, and the disappearance of jobs from small-town and rural America.

As CBS News reported:

Rural America may be at the outskirts of our national life, but it has become ground zero in terms of troop casualties. The war is taking a disproportionate toll on our rural communities. According to a study by the Carsey Institute, rural areas have suffered 27 percent of casualties but hold only 19 percent of the population. The survey also concluded that the death rate for rural soldiers, as a percentage of their hometown population, is 60 percent higher than for soldiers from cities and suburbs.[44]

The military, including the National Guard or reserve forces, can become the only choice for those who want a college education but whose families are struggling and are unable to pay as college tuitions rise and federal education funds dry up. CBS News quoted the Kerrick, Minnesota (pop. 71), farm family mother of a young soldier killed in Iraq, who said she was not surprised that so many of the US casualties in Iraq come from small towns: "I think there's a real crisis in this country the way college costs have risen. If you don't have a lot of money, the Army is a way to go to college."[45]

But many potential recruits are rejecting the military despite the lack of other opportunities, largely because of the Iraq war. The recruitment of young African Americans into the military has dramatically dropped—from a traditional level of about 25 percent of all recruits to just over half that number during the first four years of the Iraq war. The Pentagon itself admits this is in large part due to opposition to the war. Since 2003, the year the war in Iraq began, African-American enlistment has dropped more steeply than at any time since the end of the official draft exactly 30 years earlier. African-American hip-hop artists and other musicians have been among the earliest opponents of the war among black youth. But opposition goes further than that. According to Navy Commander Gregory Black, Ret., who runs the Black Military World website, "A lot of us really don't understand what this war is about. All we know is we're fighting halfway around the world—people of color."[46] Partly in response to the drop in African-American recruitment, the military has made recruitment of Latinos a top priority. Latino enlistment in the army rose 26 percent from 2001 to 2005.[47]

Both African-American and Latino communities have become central points of counter-recruitment mobilization, broadening the antiwar movement while providing young, poor, and often particularly vulnerable people of color with real information to counteract the lies and distortions of quota-driven military recruiters. In the absence of a legal draft, every recruit signs a personal contract with the military, agreeing to serve for a certain number of years, and in return the Pentagon promises a certain job category and salary, signing bonuses, training, future tuition assistance, and other benefits. According to many members of the armed forces, many of these benefits never materialize or aren't as much as they'd been led to believe. Wrenching stories abound of young soldiers ordered to return their signing bonuses after being injured in Iraq and pulled off the battlefield too early in their deployment; the army or marines didn't get their money's worth, presumably.[48]

As enlistment quotas become more and more difficult to meet, the military has been lowering the standards for enlistment. According to the National Priorities Project, of the 67,000 first-time recruits entering basic training in 2007, only about 70 percent had graduated from high school, down from 83 percent just two years earlier. According to University of Maryland military sociologist David Segal, "all of this is going to impact on the ability of the [army] to perform the mission. They are not going to perform as well in Iraq, and they are far less prepared to go anywhere else." Even more significant than education level, perhaps, is the increasing willingness to allow convicted felons into the military. Former Reagan administration Assistant Defense Secretary Lawrence Korb, noting that the Army allowed 1,620 felons to join last year, said "the Army is low-quality. … I think when you get down that low, you're broken."[49]

Whether the military is institutionally "broken" or not, what are consistently broken are the contractual agreements and commitments the US military makes, the lies it tells to its young and too often poorly educated recruits. A key component of these lies has

to do with the "stop-loss" law written into military
service contracts. The law states that if the president
determines it to be a military necessity, he or she can
order a soldier to remain in the military past the end
of the soldier's contractual end date. The advertising
campaigns run by the US military focus intensely on
the allegedly voluntary nature of enlistment. None of
the advertising, and apparently few of the recruiters
themselves, point out to vulnerable recruits that the
fine print in the back pages of the contract allows the
military to ignore the contract's terms and order the
soldier back to Iraq—or Afghanistan or Somalia or
anywhere else—regardless. The powerful 2008 film
Stop-Loss tells the story of the consequences of this
policy, what is often called a "back-door draft." It is
largely through stop-loss forced reenlistment, along
with the continual deployment of National Guard and
Reserve troops who initially joined the military to
support their local communities in times of national
emergency, that the Bush administration has managed
to maintain the 150,000-plus troops in Iraq
throughout the war, all the while trumpeting the
values of a "volunteer" military.

It remains unclear how long the current military—
weakened by casualties, diminished by losses of those
eager to leave an unpopular and unwinnable war, and
faced with fewer and less capable recruits, can sustain
its over 150,000-troop occupation of Iraq. Some
trained soldiers are returning to Iraq as private
military contractors after their military term ends,

rationalizing the danger with the huge rise in salary, but expanding even further the already dangerous reliance on outsourcing the war. If US policymakers and a post-Bush administration move to deploy more troops to expand the US–NATO occupation of Afghanistan, let alone if there is an effort to mobilize US troops against Iran or perhaps to challenge Russia in Georgia, the degree to which the Iraq war has damaged the US military will be even more obvious.

What are "private military contractors" and why does the US need 150,000 of them in Iraq?

Two weeks before the US invaded Iraq, then Secretary of Defense Donald Rumsfeld was still enthralled with the notion of waging war on the cheap. In what was being touted as part of a "revolution in military affairs," Rumsfeld trumpeted the idea that he could win a quick, clean, decisive war against Saddam Hussein (it wasn't against the Iraqi people, or even the Iraqi military, he claimed) with far fewer troops than top military strategists advised. When General Erik Shinseki, then chief of staff of the US Army, estimated that it would take several hundred thousand troops to invade Iraq, topple the government and military, and manage the aftermath, Rumsfeld called the estimate "far off the mark"; his deputy, Paul Wolfowitz, called Shinseki "wildly off the mark." The Pentagon estimated that something less than 100,000 US troops would be sufficient.[50] Shinseki was quickly sidelined, and soon retired from the military.

But the Pentagon was wrong. And Donald Rumsfeld was wrong. In fact immediately after the US invasion of Iraq, military officers began criticizing Rumsfeld in what soon became a chorus—though a chorus only of retired, not active-duty, generals and admirals. By early 2006, in what many called "the generals' revolt," demands were rising for Rumsfeld's resignation.

By mid-summer 2008, over a million US troops had served in Iraq—many for two, three, four, or even more deployments. And there were still insufficient troops to do the job—illegal though it was—that the White House and Pentagon had set out to accomplish. Even the back-door draft of the "stop-loss" law, which allowed the president to keep soldiers in the military against their will and after the expiration of their service contracts' obligations, could not provide enough troops. Private contractors were pulled in to fill the void. The contractors serve as mercenaries to bolster the US military in Iraq. They are paid with US tax money, either by the Pentagon or the State Department, but they are not accountable to the basic laws governing the US military, nor to the criminal or civil laws of Iraq.

Some people say that the contractors working for the US occupation forces in Iraq should not all be considered mercenaries because they are not all armed and carrying out direct military action. But in fact everything they do is part of the US mission of military occupation. Their work is designed to support and increase the capacity and lethality of the US military. Their actual jobs may be cooking, cleaning barracks, doing laundry, or driving trucks. But those jobs, not involving direct use of weapons, must be done in any war. Usually these chores are carried out by the lowest-ranking soldiers—the privates and corporals, although a few local civilians might occasionally be hired as well. But in this war, these jobs are almost all contracted out to private corporations, who hire private individuals—not even Iraqi civilians, who are not trusted, but primarily individuals from low-income countries such as the Philippines, Bangladesh, India, or elsewhere. The workers are poorly paid and often badly mistreated by the contracting corporations, whose stockholders and CEOs reap huge profits from the hundreds of millions, some of them totaling billions, of dollars in Pentagon contracts.

Then there are the officially recognized armed "private military contractors"—what are traditionally defined as mercenaries. These are the gun-toting, civilian-killing cowboys documented so powerfully in books like Jeremy Scahill's *Blackwater: The Rise of the World's Most Powerful Mercenary Army*. Those mercenaries—most of them Americans but some of them white South Africans who served in South Africa's apartheid-era police or military, or Chileans who served the brutal US-backed dictatorship of Augusto Pinochet—are highly trained, highly paid (security contractors can earn as much as $400,000 per year for the same work as a US soldier earning $40,000), and unaccountable to anyone or any laws.

One of the last regulations imposed on Iraq by US proconsul Paul Bremer on June 27, 2004, the day before Bremer left Iraq and ostensibly "transferred sovereignty" to Iraq, was Order #17, which ensured that US-paid mercenaries would not be held accountable to Iraqi law. That regulation remained in force at least as late as summer 2008 despite Iraqi parliamentary efforts to reverse it. And because they are not official members of the US military, the mercenaries also cannot be held accountable under the US Uniform Code of Military Justice for any crimes or violations they may commit. In theory they, or at least their companies, could be held liable under US civil law. But in practice they are not—there is no accountability. Scott Horton, a Columbia University Law School professor and manager of a project on the accountability of private military contractors at Human Rights First, testified before the House Judiciary Committee in June 2007 that

> the notion of immunity introduced in Order No. 17 is far more sweeping than the prior SoFA [Status of Forces Agreement] practice. It contains a blanket bar to criminal justice action in Iraq. This is particularly strange because there is no alternative arrangement made for a prosecution by U.S. authorities on Iraqi soil (such as exists, for instance, in the U.S.–Korea SoFA). It creates a situation in which removal

to the United States and prosecution in the United States is the sole alternative. Yet no such prosecution has yet occurred with respect to contractor crimes in Iraq.[51]

The use of private military contractors is motivated not only by troop shortages, but serves other goals as well. The Bush administration has spent its years in office trying not only to remake the map of the world but to remake the world's economic structures. The administration is grounded in an ideological devotion to privatization and the shrinking or undermining of the role of government. The consequences of that commitment were apparent in the aftermath of Hurricane Katrina in 2005, when government agencies that had been deliberately weakened failed to meet even the most basic needs of US citizens suffering catastrophic losses. The war on Iraq provided these pro-privatization ideologues with an opportunity to impose their theory on the core power center of any government: which meant outsourcing the US military itself.

Their ideological and political sway was powerful enough that much of the privatization campaign took place with virtually no debate in Congress, and barely any mention in the mainstream media, until the outsourcing had been consolidated, the war profiteers had made their killings, and the occupation of Iraq was moving into its fourth and fifth years. Even during the 2006 and 2008 US election campaigns, few antiwar candidates talked about the need to cancel existing contracts and bring home all the nearly 180,000 US-paid mercenaries working in Iraq.

Does calling for an end to the war mean we're not supporting the troops?

No. Real support for the troops caught up in and victimized by extremist policies from the White House and Pentagon and forced to fight an illegal war means fighting harder than ever to end the war, bring all the troops home, and take care of them when they return. The particular concerns of active-duty military members serving in the Iraq and Afghanistan wars began even before the US invaded Iraq. Military Families Speak Out, which is made up of parents and siblings of soldiers who had been or soon would be sent to these new war zones, formed in the fall of 2002, and was a visible participant in the huge February 15, 2003, global mobilizations against the war. By early 2008 over 3,700 families belonged to MFSO. Responding to the notion that somehow "supporting the troops" means supporting the war, MFSO's campaign focuses on ending financing for the war, and says "Funding the War is Killing Our Troops."

MFSO was soon followed by the creation of Gold Star Families for Peace, by those whose loved ones had been sacrificed to war in Iraq but who refused to believe that more killing would make their deaths more acceptable. Antiwar campaigner Cindy Sheehan played a major role in creating GSFP, as well as launching Camp Casey, the 2005 Crawford, Texas, antiwar encampment, named for Sheehan's son Casey, who had been killed in Iraq in 2004.

By 2006 a British counterpart to MFSO had been created and was playing an active role in antiwar mobilizations. "Military Families Against the War is an organization of people directly affected by the war in Iraq. Our relatives and loved ones are members of the British Armed Services. We are opposed to the continuing involvement of UK soldiers in a war that is based on lies," their website reads.

Iraq Veterans Against the War (IVAW) was formed as the first contingents of US troops returned home in the first year of the war. All these antiwar organizations of military personnel and their families advocate ending the war, bringing the troops home, and caring for them when they return. IVAW adds the crucial call for reparations to be paid to the people of Iraq.

And in the newest formation of military resistance, more than 2,000 active-duty soldiers, sailors, marines, and airmen have already signed the Appeal for Redress from the War in Iraq. For active-duty military personnel, direct appeal to Congress is the only form of speech not subject to military control. The appeal reads:

> As a patriotic American proud to serve the nation in uniform, I respectfully urge my political leaders in Congress to support the prompt withdrawal of all American military forces and bases from Iraq. Staying in Iraq will not work and is not worth the price. It is time for U.S. troops to come home.[52]

In early 2006, an almost unprecedented poll of US troops serving in Iraq gave the lie to the notion that all US soldiers supported the apparently unending occupation in which they were forced to take part. Although almost 90 percent still believed the popular Bush administration lie that the war was waged in retaliation for "Saddam's role in 9/11," almost three-quarters said the war should be ended within that same year. Just one in five supported Bush's call to stay "as long as they are needed." A slight majority thought their mission was clear, but even then, almost three years into the war and occupation, a full 42 percent acknowledged the US role in Iraq was still hazy.[53]

Those officials and military apologists who claim to "support the troops" are often the same ones responsible for the lack of sufficient body armor for troops sent into harm's way, for insufficient medical follow-up once soldiers leave the hospital, and especially for the appalling lack of resources to respond to the rising need for mental health treatment including post-traumatic stress disorder or PTSD, now affecting up to 30 percent of returning troops (see "What are the human, economic, and other costs to the US?"). According to a study of US troops who had been deployed to Iraq or Afghanistan conducted by the RAND Corporation, the Pentagon's own outside think tank, in early 2008:

> service members reported exposure to a wide
> range of traumatic events while deployed, with
> half saying they had a friend who was seriously

wounded or killed, 45 percent reporting they saw dead or seriously injured non-combatants, and over 10 percent saying they were injured themselves and required hospitalization. ... [T]he single best predictor of PTSD and depression was exposure to combat trauma while deployed. Researchers found many treatment gaps exist for those with PTSD and depression. Just 53 percent of service members with PTSD or depression sought help from a provider over the past year, and of those who sought care, roughly half got minimally adequate treatment.[54]

In her book *Cowboy Republic*, National Lawyers Guild president Marjorie Cohn describes how

The Bush gang frequently touts its support for our troops, some of whom are on their fifth tour of duty in Iraq and Afghanistan. But Bush issued a signing statement scoffing at the limits Congress has placed on the number of days a member of the Armed Forces may be deployed. Bush has also reserved the right to disobey congressional mandates that the Defense Secretary report to Congress about whether the prohibition against requiring injured troops to pay for their hospital meals is being enforced, and about the effectiveness of detection and diagnosis of Post-Traumatic Stress Disorder. He has likewise signed away his obligation to have his Defense Secretary institute studies about brain injuries suffered by our troops and mental health benefits for members of the Armed Forces.[55]

"Supporting the troops" by calling for an end to the illegal war that puts them in harm's way remains the clearest way of providing real support and potentially an end to the useless deaths (of both US troops and Iraqis) that continue to be the real consequences of the US war and occupation of Iraq.

Why is the US maintaining fifteen-plus bases in Iraq?

From the beginning of its invasion and occupation of Iraq, one of the US's first priorities was to build a network of military bases across the country that could quickly be used not only to stabilize Iraq and protect Iraqi oilfields and pipelines on behalf of US oil interests, but also to serve as potential jumping-off points for future US military interventions in the Middle East. A second goal was to establish an Iraqi government friendly toward the plan to maintain numerous permanent US bases in their country—as it turned out, by virtue of the government's complete dependence on US troops to maintain their power.

Along with scores of smaller military outposts, the US has constructed at least fifteen permanent bases in Iraq, including five large bases capable of holding thousands of troops. At least four of those are so large that two bus lines are required to traverse them and they resemble nothing so much as small US towns—with housing, shopping, recreation, and relaxation areas as well as military facilities. The most recent has been built less than five miles from the Iranian border—an act of almost breathtaking provocation.

There has been a great deal of misleading rhetoric and false claims from US officials regarding the bases in Iraq. Essentially, the Bush administration and far too many members of Congress simply deny that the permanent bases actually *are* permanent. At the end of 2006, the much-heralded bipartisan Baker–Hamilton Commission report on the Iraq war recommended that the president should state that the US does not seek permanent bases in Iraq. But it said nothing about dismantling the five major and numerous smaller permanent bases already in use in Iraq, and left a huge loophole allowing the US to maintain any "temporary base or bases," if requested by the (completely US-dependent) Iraqi government. In a similarly disingenuous vein, in a February 2008 *Washington Post* op-ed, Secretary of State Condoleezza Rice and Secretary of Defense Robert Gates wrote "nothing will authorize permanent bases in Iraq (something neither we nor Iraqis want)."[56]

Almost a year earlier, in April 2007, in an off-the-air conversation following a television debate, General Marc Kimmitt, then deputy secretary of defense for the Middle East, told me it was "ridiculous" to claim that the US wants permanent occupation or permanent control of its bases in Iraq. He posited Bosnia as the model, where US troops fought for a long time, but eventually pulled out and turned its bases over to the

Bosnians. "Last time I checked, General, Bosnia had no oil," I said. General Kimmitt stared at me for a moment, but had no response.

The US bases in Iraq have been officially designated "enduring"—not "permanent." The difference between these remains unclear. But the congressional efforts to rein in the bases, led by California Congresswomen Barbara Lee and Lynn Woolsey, co-chairs of the Progressive Caucus, rejected the funding of any permanent or long-term bases in Iraq. Passed into law in 2006 and 2007, the bills appear to have had no impact on actual Defense Department continuity in building and expanding unofficially permanent "enduring" bases in Iraq (including the newest base near the Iranian border).

The giant new US embassy complex under construction in Baghdad's US-controlled "Green Zone" must also be seen as a permanent military base. When finished, it will be the largest embassy in the world, supporting a staff of 5,000—the largest embassy staff in the world as well. The embassy will function as a self-contained mini-city, with its own water purification and electricity-generating capacity, housing, offices, and internally controlled access to food, commercial goods, communications, etc. Providing protection to the giant embassy and its huge staff is high on the list of pretexts for US military and political officials and presidential candidates who support leaving tens of thousands of US troops in Iraq after a partial troop withdrawal. The bases would also play a key role in the planned strategic shift in Iraq from a primarily active combat role for the 150,000 US troops and up to 180,000 mercenaries to a smaller permanent force of perhaps 35,000 to 75,000 troops whose anticipated roles would involve counter-insurgency, training, counter-terrorism, etc., and who would spend much more time on their protected bases, thus ensuring that the highest casualty counts remain Iraqi, not American.

What does oil have to do with the Iraq war?

From even before the US–UK invasion of Iraq in 2003, it was clear to many around the world that oil was the Bush administration's central motivation for going to war. The cry "no blood for oil" resonated around the world in the global mobilizations that challenged the war on Iraq even before it began.

The US has consistently claimed the "right" to control strategic resources, especially oil, across the globe. In his 1980 State of the Union address, President Jimmy Carter made clear that he deemed Persian Gulf oil part of "the vital interests of the United States of America," and that any attack on that oil "will be repelled by any means necessary, including military force."[57] Speaking at the height of the Cold War and following the Soviet invasion of Afghanistan, Carter was referring primarily to a threat to US hegemony from the Soviet Union. But the framework of maintaining US domination of the Persian Gulf would outlast the Cold War.

Power in the modern world is thoroughly bound up with strategic resources—oil first among them. But direct control of oil is not the only issue. For the US, as a global superpower, the ability to deploy troops quickly and massively to any "trouble spot" in the world, in order to crush resistance and reassert US dominion, is an equally vital goal, particularly when oil-rich territories are involved. On January 15, 1991, on the eve of launching Operation Desert Storm against Iraq, President George H.W. Bush issued his National Security Directive 54. It opened with the words: "Access to Persian Gulf oil and the security of key friendly states in the area are vital to U.S. national security. ... [A]s a matter of long-standing policy, the United States remains committed to defending its vital interests in the region, if necessary through the use of military force, against any power with interests inimical to our own."[58]

The US and the UK consistently maintained that the war had nothing to do with oil. Throughout the build-up to the war, George W. Bush and Tony Blair attempted to justify the invasion and occupation by steadfastly insisting, first, the war was about WMDs and links with terrorism, then that it was about bringing democracy to the benighted Middle East. According to Bush, it was simply a "wrong impression" that the US was interested in Iraqi oil.[59] Blair in turn claimed that "the oil conspiracy theory is honestly one of the most absurd when you analyze it. ... It's not the oil that is the issue, it is the weapons."[60]

In the last days before the 2003 invasion Bush administration officials tried desperately to convince a skeptical US and global public that oil was irrelevant to the coming war. Condoleezza Rice asserted "this is not about oil." But in the same interview she contradicted herself by claiming that the real reason for war was that the US could put the oil to better use: "The oil as it is being used now is not for the benefit of the Iraqi people. It is for the benefit of Saddam Hussein... to build palaces. And, most importantly, it is for the benefit of him to build weapons of mass destruction."[61] The denials continued. Colin Powell claimed, "this is not about oil; this is about a tyrant, a dictator, who is developing weapons of mass destruction to use against the Arab populations."[62] Donald Rumsfeld stated "it's not about oil and it's not about religion."[63]

But even before the invasion, the administration was preparing for US control of Iraq's oil industry. *Washington Post* reporter Bob Woodward documented that Bush received a secret National Security Council briefing less than a month before the 2003 invasion entitled "Planning for the Iraqi Petroleum Infrastructure."[64]

The administration's denials became even more implausible in fall 2007, when advance copies were released of a new memoir by one of the most influential figures in the US. Former head of the Federal Reserve and consummate Washington insider Alan Greenspan admitted that "Whatever their publicized angst over

Saddam Hussein's 'weapons of mass destruction,' American and British authorities were also concerned about violence in the area that harbors a resource indispensable for the functioning of the world economy. I am saddened that it is politically inconvenient to acknowledge what everyone knows: the Iraq war is largely about oil." As the London *Sunday Times* primly described it, "Greenspan, 81, is understood to believe that Saddam Hussein posed a threat to the security of oil supplies in the Middle East. Britain and America have always insisted the war had nothing to do with oil."[65]

Even those who had insisted the decision to invade was based on WMDs and terrorism had to admit that oil was still a factor. Lawrence Goldstein, president of the Petroleum Industry Research Foundation, said "if we go to war it's not about oil. ... But after Saddam, it becomes all about oil." Reflecting the same vantage point, then Undersecretary of Commerce Grant Aldonas in October 2002 pointed to potential economic advantages from war with Iraq. "It will open up the spigot on Iraqi oil, which would certainly have a profound effect in terms of the performance of the world economy for those that are manufacturers and oil consumers," he said.[66]

Presumably that was before they realized that the "profound effect" for oil consumers would be $120 per barrel oil prices, $4.00+ per gallon gasoline at pumps in the US, and an ever more desperate need to end oil dependency altogether.

Who benefits from the Iraq war?

The Iraq war has been fought at enormous financial as well as human and social cost to the United States (although of course the price the US is paying is not nearly as severe as that paid by the Iraqis). In all earlier US wars, the huge costs of war were at least partially equalized by increasing taxes on the entire population and passing stringent laws against war profiteering. The war on Iraq is the first war waged on credit— and accompanied by significant *reductions* in taxes for corporations and for the wealthiest Americans. Like any credit card company, the countries outside the US, especially China, who hold the skyrocketing US debt stand to profit significantly from interest on the continuing US war spending. In their book *The Three Trillion Dollar War*, Nobel economics laureate Joseph Stiglitz and Harvard economist Linda Bilmes identify a minimum of $616 *billion* in interest costs alone to cover current and future lending on today's war.

But those who are profiting most directly from this war are the private military contractors, the arms manufacturers, the giant multipurpose building/engineering/construction companies, and the oil companies that have seen their fortunes soar. These companies took advantage of their Washington insider connections and walked away with multi-billion-dollar contracts for wide arrays of services to the US military in Iraq. Their contracts were routinely extended despite constant cost overruns, incomplete con-struction, diversion of construction funds to bloated security budgets, and more. In 2006 Institute for Policy Studies scholar Sarah Anderson described "the Army's recent decision to reimburse Halliburton $253 million for delivering fuel and repairing oil equipment in Iraq, even though the Pentagon's own auditors had contested the bills. In a statement that did little to reassure taxpayers, an Army spokesperson explained that 'the contractor is not required to perform perfectly to be entitled to reimbursement.'"[67]

The large-scale privatization, or outsourcing, of so many of the Iraq war's military tasks has brought huge profits and escalating shareholder dividends for corporations involved in providing mercenaries to the US military. Once obscure firms such as Blackwater, CACI International, Bering Cross, and others that provide services to the US in Iraq for everything from dishwashers to bodyguards for visiting Congress members and high-ranking State Department, Pentagon, and White House officials, have become global players through their Pentagon contracts, and their stock values continue to rise.

CEO pay among the top 30 defense contractors more than doubled in the first few years after the start of the so-called global war on terror. Average total CEO compensation jumped from $3.9 million during the pre-9/11 period of 1998 to 2001 to $7.9 million from 2002 to 2005.[68] This sharp increase closely tracked with the post-9/11 boom in Pentagon contracts, which jumped from $154 billion in 2001 to

$269 billion in 2005. Average profits for the top 30 defense contractors grew 218 percent during this period, compared to 76 percent for US corporations as a whole.

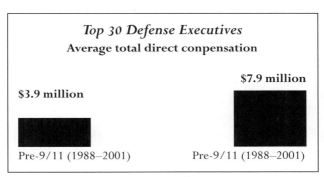

Top 30 Defense Executives
Average total direct conpensation

$3.9 million

$7.9 million

Pre-9/11 (1988–2001)   Pre-9/11 (1988–2001)

In 2006, the top 30 defense executives raked in average compensation of more than $9 million—50 times the pay of a top military general and more than 350 times the pay of a soldier on the battlefield.[69] The highest-paid CEO was Robert Stevens, head of Lockheed Martin, which in turn is the number-one recipient of Defense Department contracts. In 2006, the aerospace giant took in $26.6 billion in Pentagon contracts. In 2007, Stevens continued to garner massive bonuses, despite a scathing report from the General Accounting Office that documented more than $8.2 billion in cost overruns on two Lockheed weapons projects.[70]

Military-related pay, 2006

$25,942	$180,230	$9,095,756	$24,399,747
Army private in combat	General with 20+ years experience	Top 30 defense contractor CEOs	Highest paid defense CEO

In the first years of the war, under Republican leadership, Congress paid scant attention to war profiteering in Iraq, in stark contrast to its behavior in previous wars, World War II in particular. Anderson described how "As a U.S. senator in 1941, Harry S. Truman drove thousands of miles around the country going from one defense plant to another documenting waste and fraud. He then headed the Senate Special Committee to Investigate the National Defense Program—the Truman committee, for short. The process saved American taxpayers $15 billion (in 1940s dollars). And by uncovering faulty military equipment, he prevented the deaths of hundreds if not thousands of U.S. soldiers."[71] No 21st-century Truman Committee has yet seen the light of day. And this time around, US taxpayers and almost certainly US soldiers are paying the price.

Iraq war architect Donald Rumsfeld's vision of the war included outsourcing much of the military's work—which meant accepting war profiteering without a murmur. But Rumsfeld was not always so silent on these issues. As a Republican congressman from Illinois in 1966, he challenged the 30-year association between Halliburton's chairman and then President Lyndon Johnson. "Why this huge contract has not been and is not now being adequately audited is beyond me," Rumsfeld said at the time. "The potential for waste and profiteering under such a contract is substantial."[72]

Since the 2006 elections, the Democratic-controlled Congress has shone a slightly brighter spotlight on the war's beneficiaries. The House Oversight and Government Reform Committee, led by Representative Henry Waxman, has held several hearings and investigations into waste, fraud, and abuse, including two of the most controversial contractors—Blackwater, whose mercenaries have been involved in the killings of many Iraqi civilians, and Halliburton (where Cheney was CEO until becoming vice president), which stands accused of a long list of abuses, from overcharging the government to providing contaminated wastewater to soldiers for bathing.

But the committee's hearings have also illuminated some of the limitations on congressional power. Of the top 100 Pentagon contractors, 25 are privately held firms—which have not been required to reveal their executive pay. In 2006 alone, these companies took in a total of $16.3 billion in contracts, but we'll never know how many of those taxpayer dollars went straight into the executives' pockets. At an October 2, 2007, hearing, members of Congress pushed Blackwater CEO Erik Prince to disclose his personal pay levels. Although the company has received more than $1 billion to provide security services in Iraq and Afghanistan, Prince refused to give a specific figure, saying only that it was "more than $1 million." (In the aftermath of that hearing, Congress enacted a law that will require all major contractors in the future to reveal their executive compensation, whether they are public or privately held.)

It should also be noted that while there were a few positive developments in 2007 and 2008, for the first four or five years of the Iraq war—and until Iraqi reconstruction efforts had been largely abandoned by the Pentagon and their billion-dollar contractors—there was next to no progress in rebuilding the infrastructure of Iraq. And well into 2008, Congress had still placed no meaningful limits on how much defense contractor CEOs could personally profit from the war.

What do Americans want?

Almost 70 percent of Americans want to end the war. Americans also overwhelmingly want to somehow help repair some of the vast damage that the US war and occupation have done to Iraq and Iraqis. Many, perhaps even most, Americans want to change the role their country plays in the world. And over-whelmingly Americans want to change the dependence on foreign oil that lies at the root of so many US wars, with many committed to ending their addiction to oil itself.

Supporters of the war have often claimed that antiwar viewpoints are limited to concerns about US casualties. But in fact the highest level of opposition recorded in any national poll emerged in early November 2007, exactly at the moment that the Bush administration was trumpeting the dramatic reduction in violence in Iraq—and especially in US casualties— allegedly as a result of the "surge" that sent 30,000 additional US troops to Iraq. (Violence had indeed dropped, but it was less because of the troop surge than because of the ceasefire declared by anti-occupation Shi'a cleric Moqtada al-Sadr, and the buying off of Sunni militias into the US-backed "Awakening Councils"—both temporary phenomena not under US military control.) In that CNN poll, over 68 percent of respondents opposed the war—the highest since the war began, giving the lie to the notion that Americans were only concerned about US military casualties.[73]

Many people are rightfully concerned about the US's obligations to the Iraqi people, and don't want to "cut and run" or abandon the civilian population. That concern stems from a fundamental human response to the horror of the US war in Iraq, and most of the time comes from the best of motives. There is no question that the US owes a great debt to the people of Iraq: the US owes compensation for the damage caused by the years of economic sanctions as well as the years of war; the US owes reparations for the damage; the US owes real reconstruction support, meaning funds put in the hands of Iraqis to rebuild their country as they see fit. The question then is how to make good on those obligations.

For many American citizens, the invasion and occupation of Iraq became the linchpin not of a heroic "war on terror" but of a drive toward empire—a phenomenon long rooted in US history but characterized under the Bush administration by a reckless new escalation of unilateralism, militarism, and violations of international law. So opposition to the war shaped a broader demand that US foreign policy be rebuilt from the ground up, not just to end this war or even to end the entire so-called global war on terror wreaking such havoc from Afghanistan to Somalia to Pakistan to Gaza and potentially to Iran, but to imagine an entirely different kind of foreign policy, indeed an entirely different kind of country. Most Americans don't want to live in a rogue state striving to maintain global domination that results in increased anti-Americanism around the world, but rather in a country whose foreign policy is grounded in international law, multilateral cooperation, and environmental and economic justice—not in empire.

—PART III—

THE IRAQ WAR, THE REGION,

AND THE WORLD

How does the Iraq war affect global terrorism?

The US war and occupation in Iraq have strengthened terrorist forces—defined as those deliberately targeting civilians—in Iraq, the Middle East, and globally. Before the US invasion, Iraq was a no-go area for Islamist or any other terrorist forces; Saddam Hussein's Ba'athist government was ruthlessly secular and opposed to any religious fundamentalism. Five years into the US–UK occupation, Iraq is global center-stage for a concentrated host of terrorist forces, both Iraqi and international, most of which either did not exist or were scattered and impotent before the invasion of Iraq and the resulting destruction of its military and social infrastructure.

Iraq had nothing to do with the September 11 attacks. In fact, Iraq under Saddam Hussein had a long history of antagonism to Osama bin Laden and al-Qaeda. According to the *New York Times*:

> [S]hortly after Iraqi forces invaded Kuwait in 1990, Osama bin Laden approached Prince Sultan bin Abdelaziz al-Saud, the Saudi defense minister, with an unusual proposition.... Arriving with maps and many diagrams, Mr. Bin Laden told Prince Sultan that the kingdom could avoid the indignity of allowing an army of American unbelievers to enter the kingdom to repel Iraq from Kuwait. He could lead the fight himself, he said, at the head of a group of

former *mujahideen* that he said could number 100,000 men.[74]

Even though the size of the force was undoubtedly exaggerated, bin Laden's hostility toward secular Iraq was clear.

The war against Iraq has placed Americans in greater danger. Across the Middle East, anti-American feeling was already widespread due to US military, financial, and diplomatic backing of Israel's occupation of Palestinian land, and US support for corrupt and repressive regimes across the Arab world from Egypt to Saudi Arabia to Jordan to the little petro-states of the Arab Gulf. That was true before the Iraq war, but the war exacerbated this feeling with its constant visual brutal reminders of how US power is being deployed against Arabs and against Muslims in Afghanistan, Somalia, Pakistan, Gaza and the West Bank, potentially in Iran—and especially in Iraq.

The American public has clearly stated that the Iraq war has made their country—and Americans in general—less safe. In a July 2005 poll, nearly half of the public said that the war in Iraq has hurt the effort against terrorism. And 45 percent understood that the war has increased, not diminished, the chances of terrorist attacks in the US.[75]

US military and intelligence officials agree with the popular view. According to retired Marine General Anthony Zinni, former commander of the US Central Command, "the U.S. action in Iraq has failed to stabilize the country, and moreover, has severely damaged America's reputation in the region and around the world."[76] A national intelligence officer for transnational threats at the CIA, said that the Iraq war has given terrorists "a training and recruitment ground and an opportunity… to enhance their technical skills."[77] Others at the CIA agree. Their assessment acknowledged that Iraq may prove to be an even more effective training ground for Islamist extremists than Afghanistan was.[78]

British experts also recognize the strategic danger the Iraq war has wrought. According to the prestigious International Institute for Strategic Studies in London, the Iraq war has "accelerated recruitment" for al-Qaeda.[79] Experts at the nonpartisan London think tank Chatham House described how the Iraq war "gave a boost to the al-Qaeda network's propaganda, recruitment and fundraising, caused a major split in the [trans-Atlantic] coalition, provided an ideal targeting and training area for al-Qaeda-linked terrorists and deflected resources and assistance that could have been deployed to assist the Karzai government [in Afghanistan] and to bring bin Laden to justice."[80]

How does the Iraq war affect what is known as Islamic fundamentalism?

Contrary to much US and British propaganda, very few anti-American or anti-Western Islamist agitators, whether violent or not, are mobilized against—or even particularly interested in—"our freedoms." They may or may not share Western definitions of social freedoms, but they tend to be far more concerned about how US policy limits *their* freedom, particularly their freedom from foreign occupation in *their* countries. The US invasion of Iraq and the years of war and occupation that followed have provided important new grist for mobilizing Muslims against the seemingly endless expansion of US attacks on and wars against Islamic countries and Muslim peoples. This has led to escalations of opposition to US policies, as well as a rise in attacks on US military or political interests abroad, and sometimes terrorist attacks on perceived US- or UK-linked or other Western civilian targets.

Much has been made of the presence in Iraq of foreign Islamist fighters (mostly non-Iraqi Arabs) among the resistance and the al-Qaeda–type terrorist forces there, particularly in light of Bush's claim that these are permanent enemies of the US, experienced terrorists who have been gathering in Iraq to continue their longstanding fight against the US. A very different reality was exposed in separate studies commissioned by the Saudi Arabian government and by an Israeli think tank, both of which determined that the vast majority of these foreign fighters are not in fact former militants but became radicalized by the war itself. According to the *Boston Globe*, "the studies, which together constitute the most detailed picture available of foreign fighters, cast serious doubt on

President Bush's claim that those responsible for some of the worst violence are terrorists who seized on the opportunity to make Iraq the 'central front' in a battle against the United States." The Saudi study indicated most of these fighters were new recruits

> heeding the calls from clerics and activists to drive infidels out of Arab land, according to… Saudi investigator Nawaf Obaid, a U.S.-trained analyst who was commissioned by the Saudi government and given access to Saudi officials and intelligence. A separate Israeli analysis of 154 foreign fighters compiled by a leading terrorism researcher found that despite the presence of some senior Al Qaeda operatives who are organizing the volunteers, 'the vast majority of [non-Iraqi] Arabs killed in Iraq have never taken part in any terrorist activity prior to their arrival in Iraq. Only a few were involved in past Islamic insurgencies in Afghanistan, Bosnia, or Chechnya,' the Israeli study says. Out of the 154 fighters analyzed, only a handful had past associations with terrorism, including six who had fathers who fought the Soviet Union in Afghanistan, said the report, compiled by the Global Research in International Affairs Center in Herzliya, Israel.[81]

What is Israel's role in the Iraq war?

In the run-up to the invasion of Iraq, Israel was the

only country in the Middle East and one of very few in the entire world that supported the US plan. It would be a mistake to say that Israel and the pro-Israeli lobbies (the traditional Jewish and newer right-wing Christian Zionist lobbies) in the US drove an unwilling US to war in Iraq; the initiative for war came from the right-wing neoconservative center of the Bush administration. Most of those officials viewed Israel primarily in the context of their goal to consolidate ever-greater US dominance in the Middle East, which required a powerful, expansionist, nuclear-armed Israel as a reliable junior partner. Most Israeli military, intelligence, and political leaders had for many years viewed Iran as more threatening to Israeli security than Iraq, since those officials, unlike their US counterparts, recognized the degraded state of Iraq's military since the 1991 Gulf War and the decade of sanctions that followed.

But a US invasion and overthrow of any powerful Arab country is always applauded as innately positive in Israel. The Bush administration's longstanding fixation with Iraq also led Israel and its lobbies in the US to support that war in hopes of a follow-up war against Iran.

Years before the Bush administration came into office, many of its neoconservative hawks, including Pentagon officials Richard Perle, Douglas Feith, David Wurmser, and others, had outlined a vision of a US-dominated Middle East with Israel as Washington's strategic junior partner. Drafted originally as a campaign manifesto for right-wing Binyamin Netanyahu during his run for Israeli prime minister, "A Clean Break: A New Strategy for Securing the Realm," published by the Study Group on a New Israeli Strategy Toward 2000, of the Institute for Advanced Strategic and Political Studies, set out a regional "overthrow and remapping" plan remarkably similar to the Bush administration's own policies regarding Iraq. Within hours of the September 11 attacks in 2001, Netanyahu had described those terrorist attacks as "very good."[82] More than six years later, in April 2008, according to the Israeli newspaper *Ma'ariv*, Netanyahu reiterated that Israel was "benefiting from one thing, and that is the attack on the Twin Towers and Pentagon, and the American struggle in Iraq." He added that the 9/11 attack and the Iraq war had "swung American public opinion in our favor."[83]

Even before the Iraq war began, the US was already collaborating with the Israeli military, trying to learn as much as possible from the Israeli "model" of how to occupy an Arab country. In April 2002, Israeli troops re-invaded and reoccupied the cities of the West Bank and Gaza. In one particularly brutal operation, using tanks, helicopter gunships, and armored bulldozers, the Israeli Defense Force (IDF) took over the Jenin refugee camp in the northern West Bank. According to Amnesty International, Israeli troops deliberately denied access to wounded civilians, bulldozed or destroyed hundreds of buildings, and killed dozens of civilians including seven women and nine children.[84] Human Rights Watch investigators concluded that the Israeli military "committed serious violations of international humanitarian law, some amounting prima facie to war crimes."[85]

Instead of condemning the violations, the US used the invasion of Jenin as a model for the urban warfare they were anticipating in Iraq, and Pentagon officials met with Israeli officers to learn their tactics. According to Alex Fishman, military analyst for the bestselling Israeli daily newspaper *Yedioth Ahronoth*, the US troops in Iraq "have good teachers: the allies that they so very much do not want to mention by name."[86] Less than a year into the US occupation of Iraq, an Israeli military expert traveled to the US Marine Corps' Camp Lejeune in North Carolina to lecture US military officials on the urban warfare that had taken place in April 2002 in Jenin. Describing US efforts to model their Iraq tactics on Israel's occupation in the West Bank and Gaza, Martin Van Creveld said, "They are already doing things that we have been doing for years to no avail, like demolishing buildings... like closing off villages in barbed wire. ... The Americans are coming here to try to mimic all kinds of techniques, but it's not going to do them any good."[87] Fishman added that US military personnel had gone to learn lessons in Jenin as well.[88] Exactly two years after Israel's 2002 assault on Jenin, US troops applied the lessons they'd learned there in their attempt to pacify Fallujah. That city of 300,000 was bombed and besieged, causing severe shortages of food and medicine. At least half of the roughly 600 civilians killed were women and children.[89] The similarities to Jenin were striking—and not coincidental.

So rehearsals for the Iraq war were underway under Israeli tutelage almost a year before the war had officially been announced by the White House or voted on by Congress.

Once war in Iraq began, collaboration between the Pentagon and the IDF increased. Certainly the US military had plenty of experience in invading and occupying other countries; it didn't need help from Israel for that. But there was a recognition in Washington that Israel's particular history of a long occupation of an Arab population, along with its specific familiarity with means of exploiting cultural and religious (i.e., Arab and Muslim) sensibilities in the context of arrest and interrogation would be of special value to US troops. As a result, the Pentagon arranged for Israeli commandos to train US special forces troops at Fort Bragg, NC. The IDF taught the US troops skills they had honed during their almost forty years of occupation of the Palestinian West Bank, Gaza Strip, and East Jerusalem, including urban warfare, nighttime raids, and assassinations.

US troops also traveled to Israel to train in joint exercises. Brigadier General Michael Vane, deputy chief of staff of the Army Training and Doctrine Command, admitted that the troops had visited a model Arab town used for training Israeli troops in how to occupy Palestinian towns. The purpose, he said, was "to glean lessons learned from their [Israel's] counter-terrorist operations in urban areas." According to Israeli officials,

> in fighting insurgents in Iraq, the United States is drawing on some of Israel's methods and experiences in the West Bank and Gaza Strip, including running checkpoints and tracking militants with drone aircraft. ... Recent U.S. methods in Iraq increasingly mimic those Israel uses in the West Bank and Gaza—setting up impromptu checkpoints, keeping militants on the defensive with frequent arrest raids and, in at least one case, encircling a village and distributing travel permits. An Israeli security official, speaking on condition of anonymity, said Israel has briefed the U.S. military on its frequent use of drones, or unmanned reconn- aissance aircraft.... Israel uses drones to monitor targeted killings, often helicopter missile attacks on fugitives' cars. Israel has killed at least 117 terror suspects and 88 bystanders in targeted attacks.[90]

For years, even while the Pentagon was conducting joint training exercises and otherwise collaborating with the IDF, the US still officially criticized Israel's assassination strategy in the occupied territories. It never did anything to actually pressure Israel to stop it, but it formally distanced itself from assassination-as-policy. That prim distancing stopped in late 2002, only months before the US invasion of Iraq, when Israel's assassination policy was endorsed both by Bush and then Democratic presidential candidate John Kerry.

A year later, reports surfaced that US covert military squads posing as Arabs might be carrying out Israeli-style "targeted assassinations" in Iraq. In December 2003 Seymour Hersh wrote about those assassinations in the *New Yorker*, and in a follow-up piece in the British *Guardian*, Julian Borger quoted a former US intelligence official talking about Iraq. "This is basically an assassination program. That's what's being conceptualized here. This is a hunter-killer team." The official goes on, "It's bonkers, insane. Here we are. We're already being compared to [then Israeli Prime Minister Ariel] Sharon in the Arab world, and we have just confirmed it by bringing in the Israelis and setting up assassination teams." The official goes further to say that Israeli "consultants" have not only been at Fort Bragg but also in Iraq with US troops.[91]

Israeli models were not only used in fighting, but in interrogation techniques. Israeli prison and interrogation policy provides a clear model for what became public scandals in Abu Ghraib, Guantánamo, and other US prisons during the Iraq war. Israeli Facility 1391 is a secret prison where due process is nonexistent and inmates can essentially disappear. According to Israeli human rights activist Manal

Hazzan, "our main conclusion is that it exists to make torture possible." Since it opened more than two decades ago, Palestinians have disappeared into the prison, and are routinely held in tiny darkened cells without any information as to where they were, how long they will be held, and with lawyers, family, and the Red Cross denied access. They have been kept hooded, stripped naked for constant interrogation, and subjected to sexual humiliation and sexual torture. It sounds like a template for Abu Ghraib and Guantánamo. Even Israel's former intelligence chief, Ami Ayalon, said "I don't think today, that such an institution should exist in a democracy."[92] Some US military and intelligence officials said the same thing about Guantanamo and Abu Ghraib, and were also ignored.

Ultimately, the lessons from Israel will likely fail to provide a winning strategy for the US occupation of Iraq. But from its origins the Iraq war has been linked to US support for Israeli occupation. US requests for Israeli military training and advice have served only to consolidate US support for Israel's own occupation strategy. In this context, the Iraq war results in ever-greater US support for Israel's violations of international law. The war has set back even further the goal of real, permanent, comprehensive, and just solutions to the Israeli–Palestinian conflict, which require an end to the Israeli occupation, and thus to US support for the occupation, as the first step.

What is Iran's role in the Iraq war?

Iran and Iraq share not only a long border but a long history of involvement. Competition for regional domination between the two large, powerful, oil-rich countries goes back a long way; that competition culminated in the Iran–Iraq war that raged throughout the 1980s (exacerbated by US military assistance to both sides). The two countries are different in many ways—Iran is majority Persian, Iraq majority Arab; Iranians speak Farsi, Iraqis speak Arabic; and the two have very different histories. But they have much in common as well: populations of both are overwhelmingly Muslim and both have Shi'a majorities, who travel between the countries to reach Shi'a holy sites. Each country includes numerous smaller minority populations who have faced varying levels of inequity and integration in different periods; in both countries the Kurdish communities have suffered consistent discrimination.

Throughout the years of Saddam Hussein's Ba'athist rule, many Iraqis, primarily Shi'a who later created Shi'a-defined political parties, sought refuge in Iran. By the time they returned to Iraq after the US invasion in 2003, many had lived in Iran for decades, had studied and opened businesses there, had married Iranians and sent their children to Iranian schools. After the invasion and throughout years of US occupation, Iraq remained Iran's second-largest export market for all goods other than oil. And trade continued to rise. In 2006 Iran sold $1.3 billion worth of goods to Iraq, and the Congressional Research Service estimated that 2007 non-oil trade would reach $2 billion.[93]

Not surprisingly, the government in Iran remains influential among Iraq's post-invasion pro-occupation government officials and other elites, many of whom were among those Iraqis who spent years of exile in Iran. Iran was one of the first countries in the region to recognize the occupation-backed government of Prime Minister Nuri al-Maliki, and remains one of the few to maintain full-scale diplomatic relations with Baghdad. Equally unsurprising, Iran also remained influential among other Iraqis, especially Shi'a, who opposed the invasion and continued to fight against the occupation. Moqtada al-Sadr, a powerful Shi'a cleric and scion of an influential religious family who is known for his and his supporters' opposition to the US occupation and his command of the Mahdi Army militia, spends part of his time studying and burnishing his religious credentials in Qom, Iran's religious capital.

There is no question that Iran has an interest in preventing the violence and instability in Iraq from spilling over its border. But since the US overthrew the government and seized control of Iraq through its 2003 invasion and occupation, Iran also remains the one country capable of challenging US hegemony in the oil-rich and strategic Middle East. The Bush administration was not prepared to allow that potential challenge to exist. Beginning in early 2006, about the same time that sectarian violence and US military casualties were reaching their height in Iraq, escalating rhetoric against Iran began emanating from the White House, indicating that a US military attack on Iran—however dangerous the consequences—was a real possibility.

Throughout 2006 and much of 2007, the Bush administration's focus was on ratcheting up sanctions against Iran based on Iran's alleged nuclear weapons program, despite the fact that the International Atomic Energy Agency (IAEA), the UN's nuclear watchdog agency, consistently denied any evidence existed, and that the administration's own National Security Estimate (NIE) of December 2007 had confirmed that Iran had no nuclear weapons program. The NIE represented the consensus view of all sixteen US intelligence agencies.

By mid-2007 it became clear that the nuclear weapons claims were not sufficient to build the kind of domestic and international support the Bush administration wanted to bolster its threats against Iran. Global suspicions remained regarding the unsubstantiated US claims about Iran's nuclear weapons program because of the Bush administration's similar lies in the run-up to the invasion of Iraq. But it became clear that the Bush administration—at least some of its key figures—were determined to build support for attacking Iran. Deliberate provocations began, including sending US aircraft carriers and other warships to the Persian Gulf, launching major military exercises off Iran's coast, and threatening a US military attack when Iran captured a British navy ship in the Persian Gulf and held fifteen British sailors for almost two weeks before releasing them unharmed. Israel joined the fray, raising its own threats to attack Iran if the US didn't.

Other provocations included US troops in Iraq kidnapping five Iranian diplomats working at the request of the US-backed Iraqi government and holding them in violation of their diplomatic immunity; the US arrested and held other Iranian civilians in Iraq as well. In February 2007 Bush gave his Iraq commanders explicit orders to kill or capture Iranians in Iraq.[94] Construction began on a large new US military base in Iraq less than five miles from the Iranian border.[95] By summer 2007 the Bush–Cheney strategy had shifted to a new pretext, instead of backing down from their "Iran is making nuclear weapons" claim once the NIE had proved it false. They began to focus on the role Iran was playing inside Iraq as the next rationale for continuing to threaten Iran. Pentagon briefings began to use language deliberately designed to inflame US public opinion, accusing Iran of being responsible for killing American soldiers in Iraq. General Petraeus's high-profile testimony to Congress in September 2007 led the charge, claiming that Iran "seeks to turn the Shi'a militia extremists into a Hezbollah-like force to serve its interests and fight a proxy war against the Iraqi state and coalition forces in Iraq."[96]

In January 2008, when the Maliki government, backed by US air strikes and other assistance, launched a major attack on supporters of Moqtada al-Sadr in the southern oil city of Basra, much Bush administration and US media attention focused on accusations that the resistance militants had used what US officials claimed were Iranian arms. In contrast, little attention was paid to the fact that after a week of brutal fighting, with Maliki's military losing, Iran stepped in to negotiate a ceasefire that ended the fighting. The fighting in Basra also pointed out that the highly acclaimed reduction of violence in Iraq from early spring through November 2007 had long since leveled off, and by early 2008 attacks and casualties—Iraqi and American—were on the rise again.

By April 2008 even the *New York Times* was showing its skepticism. In a front-page article the *Times* acknowledged that despite Bush administration claims:

> It remains difficult to draw firm conclusions about the ebb and flow of Iranian arms into Iraq, and the Bush administration has not produced its most recent evidence. But interviews with more than two dozen military, intelligence and administration officials showed that while shipments of arms had continued in recent months despite an official Iranian pledge to stop the weapons flow, they had not necessarily increased. Iran, the officials said, has shifted tactics to distance itself from a direct role in Iraq.[97]

But in a trajectory virtually indistinguishable from the run-up to the war in Iraq in 2002–2003, skepticism even in high places had little impact on the the Bush administration, whose choir was belting out the same tune. The same day as the *Times* article appeared, the chairman of the Joint Chiefs of Staff, Admiral Michael Mullen, again blamed Iran for "increasingly lethal and malign influence" in Iraq, and confirmed that the Pentagon actually was planning "potential military courses of action" in Iran.[98] CIA Director Michael Hayden, citing simply "my opinion," asserted that "it is the policy of the Iranian government, approved to highest level of that government, to facilitate the killing of Americans in Iraq."[99]

Some observers had hoped that the less ideologically driven Secretary of State Condoleezza Rice might resist the pull of the most extreme militarists in the administration. But on April 28, 2008, Rice matched the harshest rhetorical attacks on Iran, outlining for the American Jewish Congress a scenario in which the entire, broadly defined Middle East was "suddenly" riven by regional conflict—a conflict that had nothing to do with the US war in Iraq, with the US–NATO war in Afghanistan, with Israel's occupation of Palestine, but was somehow created only through Iran's malign influence. "[O]f deepest concern," Rice said, "the leaders of Hamas are increasingly serving as the proxy warriors of an Iranian regime that is destabilizing the region, seeking a nuclear capability, and proclaiming its desire to destroy Israel." She described a new "belt of extremism" including Hamas, Hezbollah in Lebanon, anti-occupation militants in Iraq, and "radicals even increasingly in places like Afghanistan." The fact that all of that was "supported overwhelmingly by Iran and to a certain extent Syria, but particularly Iran," Rice claimed, "gives this conflict a regional dimension it has not had before."[100]

With that level of rising unity across the Bush administration, the danger of expanding the Iraq war into Iran could hardly be greater. As US politics moved inexorably into the 2008 electoral season, the question of expanding the Iraq war into Iran remained close to the top of the media and candidates' agenda. Republican candidate John McCain made his willingness to attack Iran abundantly clear: answering a supporter's question of what he would do, he smiled and sang out new words to the 1960s-era Beach Boys tune "Barbara Ann." His lyrics were "Bomb bomb bomb, bomb bomb Iran…" It was greeted with great applause. Democratic candidate Barack Obama focused on a commitment to open direct talks with the Iranian leadership, although he too reasserted that "all options" remain on the table.

In the meantime, Iran remains a major player within Iraq. Whatever its role in arming Shi'a militias, Tehran retains close ties to the Iraqi government, key political parties, and influential Iraqi religious leaders, and continues to be Iraq's largest trading partner. These realities will long outlast the Bush administration.

Whether officials are prepared to acknowledge them or not, Washington will likely continue to maintain ties, however unofficial and deniable, with Tehran in the shared interest of keeping Iraqi violence from spreading outside its borders.

Do Arab and other governments in the region support the Iraq war? What about Arab people?

In the run-up to the 2003 US invasion, no Arab government openly backed the US drive toward war. The Arab League voted unanimously, except for Kuwait, against an invasion of Iraq.

Even Kuwait, a close ally of and strategically dependent on the US, as well as the target of Iraq's invasion and brief occupation in 1990–1991, did not officially support the US plans until the moves toward war were almost complete. Of course by the time the invasion was about to be launched, key US allies in the region came under even greater US pressure to back the attack.

Saudi Arabia refused to officially support the invasion, although by fall 2002 it had quietly agreed to allow the Pentagon to use bases in the country as staging grounds for attacking Iraq, even while claiming publicly that it would only allow this if the US and the UK won a second UN Security Council resolution explicitly approving military action. The Saudi ambiguity showed the competing pressures facing the kingdom: a virtually complete military and strategic alliance with the US and therefore an eagerness to provide whatever Washington wanted, while at the same time having to maneuver around massive public opposition not only in Saudi Arabia itself but across the Muslim world in order to maintain legitimacy for the Saudi kingdom as defenders of Islam's holiest sites. Although the monarchy in Riyadh had little concern about the views of its citizens, it was not eager to inflame public opinion to a degree that might actually threaten the stability of the house of Saud and its absolute control over Saudi Arabia and its oil.

Further, the Saudi royal family remained uneasy about the potential consequences of a US–UK invasion of Iraq and overthrow of the Ba'athist regime. The most likely results were understood even then: any new Iraqi government was likely to be Shi'a-dominated and likely to build (or continue) strategic ties with Iran, which would become an unchallenged regional power with the demise of its longstanding opponent, the government of Saddam Hussein. For Saudi Arabia, and most of the Saudi-backed, oil-rich, and US-dependent micro-monarchies of the Gulf, such an outcome was nothing to look forward to. So the Saudi agreement to provide the Pentagon with base rights was a quiet, grudging deal that the Riyadh royals desperately tried to keep out of the media.

It should be remembered that covert Saudi backing of US military actions in the Middle East is hardly a new story. Since the end of the 1991 Gulf War against Iraq, tens of thousands of US troops had been based in Saudi Arabia, launching patrols and bombing raids in the southern "no-fly" zone in Iraq, and spawning the outrage of Osama bin Laden and others who saw the US military presence in the kingdom as sacrilegious.

The smaller Gulf states were similarly cautious. Qatar and Bahrain, both of which had allowed a long-term US military presence in their countries beginning during the 1991 Gulf War, publicly opposed a US invasion and supported diplomatic solutions instead. Qatar is the home base of the pan-Arab satellite television network al-Jazeera, known for its blistering, critical coverage of the US threats and later the US invasion and war in Iraq, so its claimed opposition to a US invasion had some logic. But shortly after the September 11, 2001, attacks, the Pentagon began moving much of its regional command center from Saudi Arabia to Qatar, and by September 2002 the US Central Command had set up shop in Qatar as well. Bahrain had served as a base for the US Navy in the Middle East since the 1970s, and as headquarters for the Navy's Fifth Fleet since 1995. So Qatar's and Bahrain's rhetorical opposition was understood as reflecting their own need to placate potential domestic opposition, not as serious resistance.

Syria opposed the invasion from the beginning, and used its position as a non-permanent member of the United Nations Security Council in 2002 and 2003 to vote against any endorsement of the US–UK calls for war. Egyptian President Hosni Mubarak traveled around the Arab world seeking support for pressuring Iraq to admit UN weapons inspectors back into the country, hoping that would placate the US war planners. Egypt, of course, was and remains the second-largest recipient of US foreign aid after Israel. Jordan, a long-time US ally and dependent, followed Saudi Arabia's lead in publicly opposing but secretly backing the invasion. King Abdullah was one of the more public Arab voices cautioning against war and urging that diplomacy be allowed to run its course. In the summer of 2002 Abdullah told the *Washington Post* that any attempt to invade Iraq would be a "tremendous mistake" and that it could "throw the whole area into turmoil."[101] Concerned about potential unrest in his country, where 60 percent of the population are Palestinian refugees, Abdullah urged Bush to focus instead on solving the Palestinian–Israeli conflict. But at the end of the day he accepted the US–UK invasion with little hesitation.

Surprisingly, it was Turkey, a NATO member and close US ally, that proved willing to stand up to the US and refuse to provide Washington with the assistance it wanted. Turkey was uneasy about war in Iraq, as it had long feared the rise of an independent or even a more powerfully autonomous Kurdish state in northern Iraq, seeing this as likely to spur renewed independence demands among Turkey's own Kurdish population. For more than a decade Turkey had opened its Incirlik air base to US and British planes patrolling and sometimes bombing in the so-called no-fly zone in northern Iraq. Now Washington wanted to use Incirlik as the key launching ground for invading Iraq from a second front in the north. The Turkish government, concerned about maintaining US support for Turkey's entry to the European Union, was eager to comply; the government agreed immediately, even before the official US decision to invade had been announced. Public opposition skyrocketed, at various points including 90 percent of the Turkish people. In January 2003 Turkey's government, trying to buy off public opinion and avert a vote of no-confidence, convened a regional conference aimed at averting a US invasion of Iraq. The conference stated that "military strikes on Iraq might further destabilize the Middle East." But public opinion continued to oppose Turkish involvement in Washington's war, and less than three weeks before the US–UK invasion, the parliament of the reasonably democratic Turkey rejected the government's proposal to allow US and British planes to use the Incirlik base to attack Iraq. Parliament never backed down, and the US–UK military plans had to be redrawn to eliminate their anticipated second front, preventing an invasion of Iraq from the north.

What characterized the regional response to the invasion of Iraq more than anything else was the powerful unanimity of public opinion. Across the absolute monarchies and family-run military states of the Arab Middle East, protestors poured into the streets of capitals usually immune from such pressures.

While few Arab leaders had much concern for public sentiment, there was growing unease in a number of countries that public outrage could threaten their regimes' carefully cobbled together but ultimately fragile hold on power. On February 15, 2003, the day of global mobilization when "the world said no to war," demonstrators across the Middle East took to the streets in Alexandria, Amman, Aligarh, Baghdad, Bahrain, Beirut, Bethlehem, Cairo, Damascus, Gaza, Irbid, Istanbul, Jenin, Maan, Manama, Muscat, Nablus, Qasur, Rabat, Rafah, Ramallah, Sana'a, Sidon, Tel Aviv, Tripoli, Widhat, and more.

The hypocrisy of the Arab governments was clear. Before the invasion, the Arab League unanimously declared "total rejection of any attack on Iraq." Four days later, Algeria's independent *Al-Khaber* wrote, "Before the ink had dried on this resolution disavowing any military action against Iraq, Kuwait's ruling House of al Sabah announced their country's willingness to accept the very American troops that the Turkish Parliament had refused to accommodate on Turkish soil, which means that the House of al Sabah doesn't believe in its commitments at the latest summit."[102] Kuwait was hardly the only Arab government caught between dependence on the US and massive public opposition to the US war: Saudi Arabia, Oman, Qatar, Bahrain, the UAE, and others all provided various levels of support to the US-led invasion and occupation of Iraq.

Once the invasion was underway, and especially after the overthrow of the Iraqi government and the consolidation of the US–UK occupation, Arab governments struggled to balance the destabilizing potential of public rage with their eagerness to remain on the good side of their longtime sponsor and military protector. While the concerns of what US policymakers and the too-compliant US media called the "Sunni Arab governments" were not particularly focused on the Shi'a nature of Iran, there had always been contention between countries vying for power in the Middle East, and Iraq had for decades represented the Arab bulwark against Iranian regional power. Certainly the Shi'a populations in some Arab countries, who were generally poorer and more disenfranchised, could potentially become a threat to the stability of unpopular regimes, and the unease about possible Iranian support for those marginalized populations was real. But in the main, Arab governments' willingness to accept US demands to at least partially normalize their relations with the occupation-backed Iraqi government, and to ratchet up antagonism and threats toward Iran, was driven far more by fear of losing US support than by actual fear of Tehran.

Arab public opposition did not lessen throughout the years of war and occupation of Iraq. More than five years into the war, in spring 2008, polls in Saudi Arabia, Egypt, Morocco, Jordan, Lebanon, and the UAE found that 61 percent believed that Iraqis would figure out how to bridge their differences if the US pulled out its occupying troops. A year earlier, with the US "surge" already underway, only 44 percent took that position. And also by 2008, only 6 percent across the Arab world believed that the US "surge" had succeeded in reducing violence in Iraq. Eight out of ten Arabs surveyed believed that Iraqis were worse off in 2008 than they were before the 2003 US invasion; only 2 percent said they thought Iraqis were better off. According to Shibley Telhami at the University of Maryland, who supervised the poll, "There is a growing mistrust and lack of confidence in the United States. You see this in the number of people who are more comfortable with the US withdrawal from Iraq." He noted that in 2008 more people in the survey wanted US troops out of Iraq than in 2007. While the survey did indicate Arab concern that Iraq could remain unstable and spread instability elsewhere in the region, most of those surveyed did not view Iran as a major threat.

Perhaps most significantly, 83 percent of the population in these Arab countries—whose governments are most closely allied with the United States—held an unfavorable view of the US. Asked which world leader they disliked most, 63 percent chose US President George Bush. Only 39 percent chose Israeli Prime Minister Ehud Olmert.[103]

Isn't the Iraq war distracting the US from the real war against terrorism in Afghanistan?

Certainly the Iraq war has come at a huge cost. Putting aside the far greater price exacted on Iraq and Iraqis, the massive deployment, including the deaths and injuries, of US troops, the spending of vast sums of US tax dollars with all the inevitable economic and social consequences in the US, and the rapid depletion of the few remaining dregs of US international credibility, all are consequences of the Iraq war and occupation. It is also true that the Bush administration's focus on waging war in Iraq and threatening war in Iran has impeded its ability to find and bring to justice those actually responsible for the terrible crimes of September 11.

But it would be a mistake to think that the problem with this trade-off is that these wars have been a distraction from the so-called real war on terror as it is being waged in Afghanistan, Pakistan, and elsewhere. While the invasion and occupation of Afghanistan have not yet led to quite the same level of disastrous consequences as the war and occupation of Iraq, living conditions for ordinary Afghans remain dangerous, violent, impoverished, and desperate.

It shouldn't have been surprising that a new war in Afghanistan didn't help create stability, let alone democracy, after years of Taliban control. The Taliban forces had come to power with large-scale popular support because they were seen as being able to end the years of brutal fighting between various warlords.

Before that were the years of a Cold War proxy war between the Soviet-backed Afghan government and US-backed *mujahideen* guerrillas that included the young Osama bin Laden. More war was never likely to improve the lives of most people in Afghanistan—and it hasn't.

Just a week after September 11, 2001, with US threats to attack Afghanistan hovering, the *Los Angeles Times* front-page headline read "Afghans Teeter on Edge." The heading warned, "aid workers fear a major US offensive could trigger mass starvation in a land where millions are already suffering." Citing the UN High Commissioner for Refugees, the article was stark: "With hundreds of thousands of Afghan refugees already on the move, food supplies in their nation running out and winter just weeks away, US military action against Afghanistan could lead to mass starvation, aid agencies warned Sunday."[104]

The *LA Times* was right. The major US military attack could and did trigger mass starvation and worse. But those in the US who exploited the horror of the September 11 attacks to gather support for war were not concerned with the fate of Afghan civilians. They turned what would have been a just and legitimate effort to bring to justice the perpetrators of a crime against humanity into a slogan for justifying war half a world away.

The terrorist attacks of September 11, 2001 were unspeakable crimes—crimes against humanity. But they were not acts of war. Under the UN Charter, the use of military force is legal under only two conditions: if authorized by the UN Security Council, or in the case of immediate self-defense. Despite US claims, the October 7, 2001, invasion of Afghanistan was not authorized under Article 51 of the UN Charter, which allows a nation to use self-defense. The definition of self-defense under Article 51 is actually quite narrow. A country has the right to use force in self-defense only *if* an armed attack occurs, and only *until* "the Security Council has taken measures necessary" to deal with the problem. The Council met on September 12, passing unanimously the exact resolution the US had proposed in response to the attacks—but that resolution said nothing about going to war against Afghanistan. There was no question the Council would have approved anything the US asked for at that moment, but the Bush administration was unwilling to acknowledge the UN's authority to regulate the use of international force. The Council called for financial cooperation to track terror organizations—not war or military force. If the Pentagon had scrambled fighter jets to take down the second plane before it hit the second Twin Tower, that would have been legitimate self-defense. The US invasion of Afghanistan, weeks after the attack, was not self-defense, and thus was illegal. And bringing NATO into the picture, with European and Canadian troops freeing more US troops for Iraq, did not make the war and occupation of Afghanistan legal; despite the Kosovo precedent, NATO does not have the right to authorize war, only the UN Security Council does.

Afghanistan did not go to war against the United States. A small group of Saudi and Egyptian terrorists did. They didn't live in Afghanistan, but in Hamburg; they didn't go to flight school in Afghanistan, but in Florida. They may have been inspired by someone living in Afghanistan, but that did not give the US the right to invade Afghanistan weeks after the attack. That is not self-defense, and each death of an Afghan civilian caught under US bombs is an additional violation of the laws of war.

And violence in Afghanistan is rising against both US and NATO troops, and Afghan civilians. Neither the much-trumpeted NATO occupation force nor the less-heralded separate US occupation and counter-insurgency troops have been able to improve daily life there.

So while the illegal US invasion and occupation of Iraq have certainly diverted resources, money, and public attention away from the so-far failed efforts to find and bring to justice the perpetrators of the September 11 attacks, the also-illegal war in Afghanistan has itself served as a distraction from what would have been the legitimate effort to mobilize not military force but international cooperation to apprehend and try those guilty of such a crime.

What was the United Nations' role in authorizing the Iraq war?

As the Bush administration began publicly preparing for war in Iraq in 2002, its initial plan was to coerce the UN Security Council into endorsing the US–UK invasion. After all, there was a long precedent of US bribes, threats, and punishments successfully resulting in official Council acquiescence to, and in some cases active participation in, Washington's unilateral wars. In 1990, George H.W. Bush's administration bribed China (with long-term World Bank development aid and a post–Tiananmen Square resumption of high-visibility diplomatic engagement) so that Beijing abstained rather than vetoing Resolution 678, which legalized the US-led war against Iraq. Other Council members, including Zaire, Ethiopia, and Colombia, were bribed as well, with oil, military aid, economic assistance, and more to ensure their support. And Yemen, one of only two countries to vote against (the other was Cuba), was punished. After the vote, a US diplomat told the Yemeni ambassador "that will be the most expensive 'no' vote you ever cast." Three days later, the US cut its entire aid budget to Yemen, the poorest country in the Middle East.

The "Yemen precedent" remains alive at the UN. So it was not surprising that Washington and London believed they could use similar tactics to win support for war a dozen years later. But this time it didn't work. The Cold War was over and the US's claim to being the world's sole superpower was already leading to resistance from a few countries, as well as submission from many others. Few outside the US believed the Bush administration's claims about Iraq's nuclear program, and crucially, powerful countries including France, Germany, Russia, and China, had determined that a US–UK war against Iraq simply was not in their national interests. So the dramatic US pressure campaigns of 2002–2003 failed, not only with the more powerful Security Council members and those (like Syria) who were expected to oppose the resolution, but even with the so-called Uncommitted Six, the smaller, poorer, and US-dependent countries on the Council who ordinarily could never go head-to-head with Washington, but who this time refused to give in. So Angola, Cameroon, Chile, Guinea, Mexico, and Pakistan, despite powerful and specific US threats, all stood defiant and refused to support the US–UK resolution that would have granted the invasion of Iraq UN authorization.

That resistance led the US and UK to withdraw the resolution (a decision announced on February 15, 2003, in the midst of the massive global protests against the looming war). The result was that the March 19 invasion was completely illegal, launched without United Nations approval or authorization. Eventually even then Secretary-General of the UN Kofi Annan admitted the invasion was illegal. The fact that the UN had *not* supported the US–UK call for war has played a major role in mobilizing the global opposition to the war from the pre-invasion period to the present.

But the illegality of the war has not kept the UN out of Iraq altogether. The US pressure continued even after the invasion, and the Security Council's resistance collapsed in May 2003, just two months into the war, when it passed Resolution 1483, recognizing the US and Britain as the occupying powers in Iraq. The resolution did not, in fact, legitimize or authorize the occupation; technically the resolution simply imposed on the US and UK the legal obligations of occupying powers,

> consistent with the Charter of the United Nations and other relevant international law, to promote the welfare of the Iraqi people through the effective administration of the territory, including in particular working toward the restoration of conditions of security and stability and the creation of conditions in which the Iraqi people can freely determine their own political future.

The "relevant international laws" of course include the Geneva Conventions, which impose on occupying powers a wide-ranging set of obligations designed to protect occupied civilian populations—security, housing, clean water and food, jobs, education, and more. The occupying powers are prohibited from damaging the infrastructure or seizing control of the resources of the occupied country and are not allowed to change the existing or impose a new economic or political system.

But the US and UK ignored those obligations. Instead, the resolution was widely seen as having given a UN imprimatur to the war and occupation.

And indeed it gave virtually unlimited power to the occupiers, despite the illegality of the invasion in the first place. For example, the resolution eliminated all UN monitoring of Iraq's oil sales, giving full authority to the US and UK. It gave Iraq's oil industry the kind of legal immunity that traditionally is available only to the United Nations and to its agencies; it was unprecedented to grant such protection to a national entity.

In passing Resolution 1483, the UN provided exactly the kind of functional—if not legal—authorization of the invasion and occupation of Iraq that Washington and London had failed to achieve during their campaign throughout the fall and winter of 2002–2003. This allowed the US to regain the dominance over the organization that it had, for a historic moment, been forced to cede to the power of global antiwar public opinion and mobilization—what the *New York Times* had called "the second super-power."

Resolution 1483 did not create a clear leadership role for the United Nations in the work of helping Iraq reclaim its independence and create a truly legitimate, representative government. The resolution kept the UN subservient to and dependent on the US–UK occupation—which essentially assured its failure to be able to help Iraq regain real independence. Ultimately the resolution's core purpose—its granting of an after-the-fact and not-quite-official UN seal of approval to the US–UK invasion and occupation—was not actually rooted in international law, but to the contrary stood in stark violation of the UN's own Charter.

What has the UN done during the US–UK occupation of Iraq?

Five months after the invasion of Iraq, a huge truck bomb destroyed the Baghdad headquarters of the United Nations in the Canal Hotel. Twenty-two UN staff members, including the experienced UN troubleshooter and head of the Iraq mission, Brazilian diplomat Sergio Vieira de Mello, were killed.

A year later, former communications director for the mission and long-time UN staffer Salim Lone wrote:

> The vicious terrorist attack a year ago yesterday surprised no one working for Sergio Vieira de Mello, the UN secretary-general's special representative. Indeed, the UN chiefs of communication in Iraq had met that morning to hammer out a plan to counter the intensifying perception among Iraqis that our mission was simply an adjunct of the U.S. occupation.
>
> Little did the Iraqis know that the reality was quite the opposite: By August, the UN mission had grown very distant from the Americans. The intense early relationship that Sergio, the world's most brilliant negotiator of post-conflict crises, had fashioned with Paul Bremer, the U.S. proconsul, had already

fractured. . . . General dismay over occupation tactics aside, Sergio had already parted company with Bremer over key issues such as the need for electoral affirmation of a new constitution, and the arrest and conditions of detention of the thousands imprisoned at Abu Ghraib prison. The low point came at the end of July last year, when, astonishingly, the U.S. blocked the creation of a fully fledged UN mission in Iraq. . . . Clearly, the Bush administration had eagerly sought a UN presence in occupied Iraq as a legitimizing factor rather than as a partner that could mediate the occupation's early end, which we knew was essential to averting a major conflagration.[105]

The US occupation authority orchestrated the selection of an "interim government" in spring 2004 to replace the widely scorned US-selected "Iraqi Governing Council." The process of choosing the ministers was not democratic and did not reflect the breadth of Iraqi public opinion. To try to avoid the discrediting that had already undermined the Governing Council, the US had agreed that United Nations special envoy Lakhdar Brahimi would play a central role in choosing the interim government. But in the last weeks before the May 31 deadline for identifying government ministers, Brahimi was forced to the sidelines. As a result, the interim government, like the Governing Council before it, was a creature of the United States, not the United Nations. Brahimi acknowledged that "Mr. Bremer is the dictator of Iraq. He has the money. He has the signature. Nothing happens without his agreement in this country."[106]

Brahimi's statement came too late. His and then Secretary-General Kofi Annan's decision to acquiesce, however reluctantly, to US pressure had severely undermined the UN. Brahimi could have responded to the pressure by announcing publicly that Washington had prevented him from implementing the UN's mandate (to appoint nonpartisan technocrats to run the country and prepare for elections in 2005) and withdrawn from his post. Instead, the "interim government" was put in place with the US having final approval of members in all the top positions, but with a United Nations imprimatur and "bluewashing" of the process, providing the illusion of international legitimacy. UN credibility and legitimacy was shredded by such a submission to US power and has still not been redeemed.

In early June 2004 a new Security Council resolution endorsed the US-approved interim government that was about to take office as "sovereign," and credentialed the US-dominated occupation forces as a UN-mandated "multinational force." By claiming that when the interim government took office on June 30, "the occupation will end and... Iraq will reassert its full sovereignty," the resolution provided international cover for the continuation of the occupation and US–UK control of Iraq. And crucially, while the UN resolution named the interim government "sovereign," it denied it the authority to reverse or undo the major decisions imposed on Iraq by the US proconsul Paul Bremer, including laws privatizing Iraqi resources, denying press freedom, allowing foreign corporations to control the reconstruction process, and more.

The Security Council had been sharply divided over the resolution. France, China, and Algeria wanted Iraq to be able to block any major military mission by the US occupation forces. But Washington rejected that out of hand. Secretary of State Colin Powell said, "You can't use the word 'veto.' There could be a situation where we have to act and there may be a disagreement and we have to act to protect ourselves or to accomplish a mission."[107] As a result the final resolution gave the US-controlled "multinational force" the power Washington demanded: "the authority to take all necessary measures" in carrying out the military occupation.

The UN played a role in organizing the Iraqi elections of 2005, but with the US–UK occupation still ultimately maintaining control. Once the new "official" Iraqi government came into office, still backed by the occupation, the UN role shifted to a narrower focus on humanitarian support.

As Salim Lone wrote,

> The UN is precious—not because of its name, but because it struggles, however imperfectly, to reach global consensus on the world's critical issues. The fanatics who blew up the

UN mission dealt a severe blow to its fortunes in the Middle East. But more lasting damage is being done to the legitimacy of this irreplaceable institution by demands to obey US dictates. If it continues to bow to pressure, its capital will be squandered and its resolutions rendered weightless for large chunks of humanity. [108]

Even without UN endorsement, wasn't the invasion of Iraq really an international campaign because of the "coalition of the willing"?

On February 15, 2003, at the height of the global protests against the impending war, with 12–14 million people taking to the streets in cities around the world, Washington and London finally acknowledged that their effort to force the Security Council to authorize their planned invasion was not going to succeed. They withdrew the resolution then under discussion, announcing that any future resolution would not explicitly call for war. It was a stunning victory for the "second super-power"— global public opinion—which at that moment was united with many governments and the UN itself in rejecting the Bush–Blair plans for war.

But withdrawing the resolution did not mean that the US had given up on claims of international legitimacy, even if it couldn't gain the real thing. Diplomats were dispatched around the world to coerce, bribe, and threaten governments in order to create what the Bush administration called a "coalition of the willing." The day before the invasion, then Secretary of State Colin Powell released a list of 30 countries that he claimed had agreed to be publicly identified as members of the alliance. But according to the *Washington Post*, officials of at least one of those countries, Colombia, were apparently unaware that they had been designated as a coalition partner.

Other nations, including Hungary and the Netherlands, allowed their names to be placed on the coalition list, but at the same time reassured their outraged citizens that they would not actually support the military action against Iraq in any substantive way. Powell also claimed that another fifteen countries were part of the coalition but preferred to remain anonymous. Most of these were almost certainly the Arab regimes long dependent on the US military, but who faced massive popular opposition to a US invasion. (See "Do Arab and other governments in the region support the Iraq war? What about Arab people?" above.)

Overall, given the range of economic, political, and military leverage the US could and did bring to bear on potential coalition partners, it is actually surprising that less than a quarter of the world's governments joined. In the first days after the invasion, the administration bolstered its list with several of the tiny island states frequently used to provide cover for what would otherwise be the US-and-Israel-against-the-whole-world votes in the UN General Assembly—Micronesia, the Marshall Islands, the Solomon Islands, and a few others, to count a total of 45 countries in the "coalition."

Many governments refused to allow their support to be made public. In almost every case the reason was political—governments that supported the US war faced massive opposition, sometimes even the threat of being overthrown or at least voted out of office by mobilized antiwar populations. And even aside from the fact that coalition governments had chosen to support the US war in the face of massive popular opposition in their own countries, the coalition itself was not nearly as real or representative as the Bush administration claimed. Of the fifteen Security Council members, only Bulgaria and Spain joined. Eight of Washington's and London's new partners were NATO-wannabes, eager for US–UK support for their membership claims. The split between those European countries backing the invasion, mostly former Soviet republics and Warsaw Pact members, and the powerful countries opposing it, including Germany and France, led to Defense Secretary Rumsfeld's famous line about antiwar "old Europe" becoming irrelevant.

Ironically, the coalition claiming to fight for the "liberation" of the Iraqi people included numerous countries with dismal human rights records of their own. According to democracy and honesty ratings by Freedom House and Transparency International, eleven of the countries were "not free" or only "partially free," and more than half (24) had high levels of corruption. The US State Department's own reports concluded that in eight of the coalition countries, "the overall human rights situation remained extremely poor." In eleven (Albania, Azerbaijan, Colombia, Eritrea, Ethiopia, Georgia, Macedonia, Nicaragua, Philippines, Turkey, and Uzbekistan), the State Department noted that torture and/or extrajudicial killings were carried out by security forces.[109]

In fact, the coalition in general was designed to provide political, not military support to the US–UK invasion. Only two countries—Britain (46,000) and Australia (2,000)—provided significant numbers of troops for the invasion itself. Within two months the British deployment was reduced to 18,000 and it was down to 8,600 by the end of May 2004.[110]

Both troop contributions and even official membership in the coalition dropped precipitously in the first years of the war. Across the coalition countries, governments paid a price for supporting the unpopular war. In Spain, massive antiwar opposition was strengthened with new outrage at the government's lies in claiming Basque separatists were responsible for the Madrid train bombings of March 11, 2004, instead of acknowledging that Spanish participation in the Iraq war had precipitated an attack by al-Qaeda–linked terrorists. A week later, on the first anniversary of the invasion, the US- and UK-backed right-wing government of José Maria Aznar was defeated in the polls. Within weeks, the new government of José Luis Rodríguez Zapatero withdrew all Spanish troops from Iraq. Two years later, Bush supporter and Italian Prime Minister Silvio Berlusconi faced a similar fate when he was defeated by a center-left coalition pledged to bring Italy's troops home. By 2007 Australia's pro-war John Howard was defeated by Kevin Rudd, who pledged his first act would be to negotiate the withdrawal of Australia's last 500 troops from Iraq.

By the end of March 2008 there were fewer than 10,000 non-US "coalition" troops in Iraq; more than 40 percent were from the UK.[111] In fact there was nothing "willing" about the George Bush–Tony Blair "coalition"; it was a coalition of the coerced from the beginning. And those who backed it paid a price.

What do people and governments around the world think about the Iraq war and about the US as a result of the war?

The Bush administration launched its invasion of Iraq in 2003 with full support from Tony Blair in London and rhetorical backing from Aznar in Madrid and Berlusconi in Rome, but global public opinion was overwhelmingly opposed, and the majority of governments also rejected the false claims on which the US call to war was based. Throughout the years of war and occupation that followed, that opposition has only grown.

One year after the invasion, an international poll showed that

> discontent with America and its policies has intensified rather than diminished. Opinion of the United States in France and Germany is at least as negative now as at the war's conclusion, and British views are decidedly more critical. Perceptions of American unilateralism remain widespread in European and Muslim nations, and the war in Iraq has undermined America's credibility abroad. Doubts about the motives behind the US-led war on terrorism abound, and a growing percentage of Europeans want foreign policy and security arrangements independent from the United States. Across Europe, there is considerable support for the European Union to become as powerful as the United States.

While Americans still overwhelmingly (84 percent) believed that Iraqis would be better off after the overthrow of Saddam Hussein, already only 31 percent of Russians and only 8 percent of Pakistanis believed Iraqi lives would improve.[112]

By early 2007, international views of the US role in Iraq—and, consequently, views of the US overall—had continued to plummet. A BBC poll in 25 countries, including the US and UK, found that three-quarters of respondents disapproved of US actions in Iraq. Clearly the anger about Iraq was creating broader criticism of and antagonism toward US policies in other international areas as well. In 18 of the 25 countries polled, the percentage of people who said the US was a positive influence in the world dropped from earlier years—down to only 29 percent. Across all 25 countries, almost half of respondents said the US played a negative role in the world; 67 percent disapproved of how Guantánamo detainees were treated; 65 percent disapproved of the US role in the 2006 Israeli war in Lebanon; and 60 percent disapproved of how the US responded to Iran's nuclear program.[113] And six months later even Americans were recognizing the impact of the war on international perceptions of the United States: According to a July survey of US public opinion, almost 80 percent said the Iraq war had damaged US standing in the international community.[114] As to global views of the UK, few polls inquired, but it seemed a common perspective to view Tony Blair as Bush's "poodle," the disparaging term first coined by British antiwar campaigners. Few global media or political voices appeared to see the UK as an independent, let alone strategic, player in Iraq decision-making, instead viewing London as willing, indeed eager, to follow any US lead.

Stories abound of US citizens traveling abroad and facing unprecedented antagonism from wide ranges of people holding them accountable for the horrors of US policy in Iraq and elsewhere in the so-called global war on terrorism. The collapsing levels of international approval for the US in Iraq have even challenged the longstanding assumption that most people around the world, especially in the impoverished nations of the global south, may criticize the US but they all want to go there. The steadily rising visa and other related challenges facing foreign visitors to the US—including not only those seeking asylum but would-be students, potential investors, family visitors, and even wealthy tourists— has made "coming to America" an increasing burden, and therefore an increasingly unlikely choice. The US is paying a high price for the Iraq war and is by far the poorer for it.

—PART IV—

ENDING THE WAR

What does it mean to "end the war"?

Almost from the first moment of the US–UK invasion of Iraq in 2003, politicians and political commentators have been talking about "ending" the war. Definitions of what that means have changed depending on who was doing the talking. For George Bush and others in his administration, "ending the war" meant "winning" the war, with whatever transitory definition of victory was current at the moment. Republican congressional leaders and right-wing pundits spoke of "finishing the job," whatever that meant. Mainstream Democratic political leaders called for ending the war, but refused to define their terms. Very few have been willing to define what they meant by "ending the war."

In fact, the US does not have the capacity to end the entire complex of wars currently being waged in Iraq. The US–UK invasion and occupation are not only directly responsible for massive death and destruction across Iraq, but they set in motion a convoluted set of sectarian and civil battles, conflicts over money, oil, and power, and clashes over control of Iraq's future.

What the US and UK can do—and what they must do if Iraq is to have any hope of reclaiming its sovereignty, its unity, and its future—is to end the *occupation* of Iraq, and allow Iraq and Iraqis the opportunity to work through their own crises and end, on their own terms, their own conflicts.

A *real* end to the US war and occupation of Iraq starts with:

—withdrawal of all US, UK, and other "coalition" soldiers (not only "combat troops");

—withdrawal of all 100,000 or so non-Iraqi mercenaries working for the US in Iraq;

—closing all US bases;

—renouncing all US efforts to control Iraq's oil industry and control its government.

After the end of the occupation, US–UK obligations to Iraq and Iraqis will have to include:

—financial and asylum support for Iraqi refugees and internally displaced people;

—canceling existing contracts with US and foreign contractors and transferring the funds to Iraqi companies and institutions so real reconstruction can move forward;

—supporting (but *not* attempting to control) whatever regional or international (Arab League and/or United Nations) peacekeeping, humanitarian, or related assistance the Iraqis request;

—beginning the process of providing compensation and reparations for the years of sanctions, war, and occupation.

Isn't the US trying to get out of Iraq as soon as possible?

Beginning several years into the war, the Bush administration claimed that the US occupation is a temporary phenomenon, that "we will stand down as Iraqis stand up." It was never true. The US goals in Iraq have always been primarily about US power:

expanding the US military presence, consolidating US control of Iraqi oil, ensuring that no regional competitor (i.e., Iran) could challenge US hegemony in the region. Concerns about the Iraqi people, if they existed at all, were always a far lower priority.

This is evident in the sequence of official US goals for the invasion and occupation of Iraq. Each in turn was embraced and asserted as unequivocal truth, until it was suddenly shown to be false. So weapons of mass destruction and Iraq's alleged links to al-Qaeda and 9/11 morphed into democratization, which faded into "fighting them there so we don't have to fight them here." That soon became "achieving stability, democracy and independence" and eventually that was reduced to an effort to construct "an Iraq democratic and stable enough to hold together on its own once we leave."[115]

Similarly, there has been an ever-changing parade of "enemies," the destruction or containment of whom became the centerpiece of sequential justifications for continuing the occupation. First of course it was Saddam Hussein. Then when his government was overthrown, the target shifted to the "dead-enders" and "left-over Ba'athists" leading the insurgency. Then attention shifted to the Sunni-led resistance plus the anti-occupation Shi'a militias, especially that of Moqtada al-Sadr. Then al-Qaeda in Mesopotamia took center stage for a while, and by mid-2007 Iran had emerged as the central enemy in Iraq and the central justification of why the US must maintain its occupation.

That there will be a long-term occupation—perhaps transforming in the future into something smaller that could more politely be called a "presence"—is very much a bipartisan assumption in the US. Some members of Congress—particularly those in the Progressive, Out of Iraq, and Black Caucuses—have attempted to introduce legislation that actually would stop funding the war, bring home all the troops and mercenaries, close the US military bases, prevent expansion of the war to Iran, and more. But none of those efforts have succeeded, even during the years following the 2006 elections, which brought a Democratic majority to both Houses of Congress after an election campaign whose centerpiece was the public's demand to end the war.

The occupation remains bipartisan. Republicans mainly speak of small tactical shifts while maintaining Bush's war largely unchanged; the 2008 Republican candidate for president, John McCain, spent his entire campaign as cheerleader-in-chief for continuing the Iraq war, claiming credit for what he called the "success" of the US troop surge. The mainstream Democratic leadership, including both Congress and the leading candidates for president in the 2008 election, speaks of "ending the war"—but their definition of "ending" the war actually continues the occupation. While there are certainly important differences between the candidates, Barack Obama's call for "ending the war" was defined as withdrawing *combat* troops from Iraq, with tens of thousands of US troops remaining indefinitely in Iraq. Obama has said he would begin a phased withdrawal immediately, aiming to have all forces "out of combat operations" within 16 months. He would leave behind troops for training Iraqi forces, counter-insurgency, and protecting the US embassy and other sites.[116]

Obama has said he would not build permanent bases, but left unclear whether he would dismantle the fifteen-plus bases already built across Iraq. He has not said anything about reducing the footprint of the giant 1,000–5,000-person US embassy complex or withdrawing the 100,000 non-Iraqi mercenaries working in Iraq in support of the US military. Taken together, the "residual" military force Obama would leave behind would amount to somewhere between 35,000 and 80,000 US troops deployed in Iraq indefinitely.

Wouldn't it be irresponsible for the US to withdraw all the troops? Don't we need them to scaffold the Iraqi government, protect the US embassy, defend the bases, train the Iraqi military, protect the oil, and more?

Many Americans, Britons, and other opponents of the war are concerned that the call to end the military occupation of Iraq not become a call to abandon US and UK responsibilities to the Iraqi people. That understanding, that the US and UK are obligated to try to repair some of the damage they inflicted in launching an illegal war, is certainly a powerful example of human solidarity. In one of his most famous sound bites, then Secretary of State Colin Powell created his now-viral "Pottery Barn" analogy for Iraq: we broke it, we own it. The first part of that was certainly true: the US did "break" Iraq. But Powell's "we own it" was not a call for reparations, or compensation, or even real reconstruction support for Iraq. He used the slogan to justify keeping US occupation troops in Iraq. The view that the US needs to keep 140,000 troops in Iraq (the likely number when the partial withdrawal of "surge" troops ends in July 2008) or even keep 35,000 to 80,000 "residual" troops (the range of troops the Obama plan would leave behind) is based on the belief that the US occupation is helping bring democracy, stability, and prosperity to the people of Iraq. And that claim is simply false.

The most irresponsible plan for responding to the current debacle caused by war and occupation in Iraq is to deny there is a crisis and simply continue on the same course. The most responsible plan is to acknowledge the crisis, and move to reverse it. As an old military adage goes, "if you find yourself in a hole, first thing to do is to stop digging."

It is unlikely that the current Iraqi government would remain in power without backing by a large-scale US occupation force—it almost certainly would not have sufficient support and legitimacy among the Iraqi population to remain independently viable. Despite the election that brought this particular version of government-under-occupation into office in 2005, the vast majority of Iraqis appear to view it as simply the latest in a series of US-backed political structures masquerading as independent governments. The assertion that US troops must continue to occupy Iraq to protect a government created by the US occupation, and holding onto power only as long as the occupation continues, is an insult to the very principles of independence and sovereignty, let alone democracy.

Similarly, the idea that US occupation forces— according to various Pentagon and other analysts, anywhere from 10,000 to 30,000 troops—will be "required" to remain in Iraq to train Baghdad's military assumes the independent legitimacy of those Iraqi forces. To many Iraqis and many outside observers, the Iraqi army, despite being armed, trained, and funded by the US, functions essentially as just one more militia among the plethora of armed groups contributing to the instability in Iraq; it's simply the largest among them, controlled (more or less) by Prime Minister Maliki and his Dawa Party. Ending the militarization of politics will be one of the long-term challenges facing Iraq: almost all the largest and most influential Iraqi political parties maintain powerful militias accountable to party leadership. After the end of the US–UK occupation, a truly independent and truly sovereign Iraqi government may indeed need assistance with military or police training to create a truly national security apparatus, and the United Nations, along with neighboring countries, the Arab League, or other regional forces, will be well positioned to provide that training.

The construction of the largest embassy compound in the world—indeed the largest in history—to provide US-style housing, office space, recreation, military venues, and more for what is anticipated to be an embassy staff of 1,000 to 5,000 people, creates an inevitable "necessity" for thousands more US troops to protect that compound. But an embassy truly functioning as an embassy—meaning representatives of a *different* government, not a giant governing-by-proxy institution—does not require 5,000 or even 1,000 diplomats, and does not need a giant complex designed to provide its population with electricity, water purification, food, and all services independent of those available to any ordinary Iraqi. Any ordinary embassy, staffed by an ordinary-sized team of diplomats, would be protected by State Department (US Marine-based) security; it would not require the deployment of thousands of troops. The huge new embassy and its small-town–sized population will continue to demonstrate to the world the non-sovereignty of the Iraqi government and the US's clear intention of maintaining permanent control of the country. And in turn, the end of the US occupation, including the withdrawal of all troops and mercenaries, would go very far in transforming the embassy, now a vulnerable target for anti-occupation forces, into an ordinary place of business. Those who believe the Bush mantra that the Iraq war is about stopping terrorism should remember the words of al-Qaeda leader Osama bin Laden, who spoke of the obvious reasons why his terrorist forces have not attacked Sweden. The Swedish embassy in Baghdad has still not been attacked.

Similarly, the notion that massive US troop deployments are required to "protect" existing US military bases assumes that those bases (whether they are disingenuously known as "enduring" bases or acknowledged as permanent) have a legitimate right to remain in Iraq, let alone a useful role there. Their history demonstrates the opposite. The newest of the Pentagon's oversized "enduring" bases, in fact, the giant base constructed less than five miles from the Iranian border, puts Iraq and Iraqis even closer to the center of Washington's dangerous provocations toward Iran.

The US does not have a legitimate need to "protect" Iraq's oil when the goal of that "protection" is actually to preserve US, not Iraqi, control. The US does not have a legitimate need for a 5,000-person embassy staff because normal diplomatic relations should be based on exchange of ideas and support, not imposing a shadow government in the guise of diplomacy. The US does not have a legitimate need to keep thousands of troops—"combat" troops or otherwise—in Iraq to train Iraqi soldiers because the very presence of US troops in Iraq continues to foment war and violence. And the US has no legitimate need for any military bases in Iraq, whether acknowledged as permanent or not, because those bases are not designed to protect Iraq and Iraqis but rather to maintain US military control and domination over the country and its oil.

Should we replace US and UK troops with UN Blue Helmets?

The US invasion and occupation have set in motion multiple wars inside Iraq. The end of occupation will not end all that violence—but ending the occupation is a necessary first step to allow Iraqis to begin the process of ending the internal cycles of violence. It is certainly likely that whatever governing bodies emerge after the US–UK occupation troops are withdrawn will recognize that they need international support for peacekeeping and stabilization in the traumatized country. With such a request, United Nations peacekeeping assistance, in the form of a deployment of UN Blue Helmet peacekeepers, would be a vital means of support for post-war national reunification and rebuilding Iraq's shattered social fabric.

But such a deployment must reflect the decisions and viewpoints of Iraqis themselves. To replace the current US–UK occupation with a deployment of UN Blue Helmets based on decisions by the US, or the UN Security Council, or anyone other than Iraqis themselves, would be seen by Iraqis as simply replacing one occupation with another. The United Nations would emerge again, as it did in August 2003, as the kind of target for anti-occupation resistance forces that the US and UK occupation are today.

The UN is already viewed by many Iraqis as virtually indistinguishable from the United States. Although many others in the world have forgotten, Iraqis remember that the twelve years of crippling US-led economic sanctions that decimated Iraqi society were officially imposed in the name of the United Nations. Iraqis remember that the UN's eight-month resistance to the US drive toward war in Iraq in 2002–2003 was too short, and that it collapsed in the face of US pressure to recognize the occupation. The horrific deadly assault on the UN compound in August 2003 was not a random attack, but rather was grounded in a widespread belief in Iraq that the UN was being used to legitimize the US–UK occupation—or, as Washington's then Ambassador to the United Nations Madeleine Albright once described the global institution, as a "tool of American foreign policy."

In November 2007 when the Security Council voted to extend its mandate authorizing the so-called multinational force (the US-led occupying army) in Iraq, the Council explicitly noted that the Iraqi government itself had requested, through the US, that that be the last extension of the mandate. There was some concern among a few members of the Council regarding whether the Iraqi request to extend the UN mandate might have violated the requirements of the Iraqi constitution, which the United Nations had helped craft. Article 58, Section 4, of the constitution requires ratification by parliament of all "international treaties and agreements." The Iraqi parliament had attempted to send a letter to the Council in the spring of 2007 urging them not to extend the mandate since the Iraqi government had refused to consult with or obtain ratification by the parliament, and in April 2007 a majority of Iraq's parliament had called the government's effort to extend the mandate "unconstitutional." But the US squelched any real discussion in the Council, and ultimately the mandate was extended through December 31, 2008, without the required consent of the elected Iraqi parliament.[117] The notion that deploying a replacement United Nations occupation force, against the will of the Iraqi people and against even the official position of the Iraqi parliament, would somehow solve the crisis in Iraq and end the militant resistance to occupation, was never grounded in reality.

What will Iraq's neighbors do if the US and UK pull out?

None of Iraq's neighbors wants to see the current chaos and violence in Iraq spill over their borders. Not a single country among Iraq's neighbors has an interest in keeping Iraq occupied, weak, and wracked by violence, just as none want to see Iraqis impoverished, uprooted, and fleeing their country to seek refuge in neighboring states.

That does not mean that Iraq's neighbors are pleased with the US-backed Iraqi government. Most of Iraq's neighbors—with the exception of Iran— resisted sending ambassadors or establishing full diplomatic relations with Baghdad at least well into 2008. In regional conference after regional conference, Secretary of State Condoleezza Rice and other top US officials pressured Iraq's neighbors to recognize Prime Minister Nuri al-Maliki's government, to reopen their embassies, to provide debt relief and support to the Iraqi government. But to little avail. In mid-April 2008 the *New York Times* reported on Maliki's frustration with other Arab governments for their refusal to embrace his regime. "It's hard for us to understand why our Arab brothers do not exchange diplomats with Iraq," the prime minister said. His foreign minister, Hoshyar Zebari, who spoke alongside Rice at a regional meeting in Kuwait, played the diplomat: "we have to be patient with our Arab brothers. I think the will is there—they want to reach out, and they recognize that their absence is not helpful."[118] But whether they "recognized" that or not, the Arab states were not prepared to accept an Iraqi regime with little power of its own, dependent on the US-led forces occupying its country to remain in power, and with strong ties to Iran.

Iraq is bordered by four Arab countries (Jordan, Syria, Kuwait, and Saudi Arabia) and two non-Arab countries (Turkey and Iran). All those countries' populations are predominantly Muslim. Syria is largely Sunni, but its ruling Ba'ath Party, a competing wing of the same movement that came to power in Iraq and ended with Saddam Hussein's overtthrow, is controlled largely by Alawite Muslims, a smaller breakaway sect. Saudi Arabia, whose royal family follows the extremely conservative Wahhabi branch of Sunni Islam, has a not-insignificant Shi'a population. Jordan is largely Sunni, as is its Hashemite royal family.

But other than Saudi Arabia, whose otherwise-shaky national credentials rest on being the protector of Islam's holy cities of Mecca and Medina, none of the three other Arab states define themselves primarily in religious terms. The absolute monarchies in power in Jordan, Kuwait, and Saudi Arabia were put on their thrones by the French and British colonial powers after World War I and the fall of the Ottoman Empire. The self-described credibility of each of the monarchs was grounded in various claims of their families having descended from the Prophet Mohammed. But other than Saudi Arabia, all the governments ruled in a relatively secular manner, and none identified themselves as "Sunni governments" until the US occupation of Iraq was underway.

Iraq's population is majority Shi'a; while exact figures are not available since there have been no reliable census data for many years, 55–60 percent of the Iraqi people are estimated to be Shi'a. Not surprisingly, Iraq's occupation-controlled government is dominated by Shi'a parties, ruling in a tenuous coalition with Kurdish and some Sunni parties, as well as a few much smaller nationalist or non-sectarian parties. The Shi'a parties are quite diverse, including those of Prime Minister Maliki's Dawa Party and another Shi'a party aligned with him, as well as other Shi'a parties virulently opposed to Maliki's government and the US occupation, such as the movement led by Moqtada al-Sadr. Virtually all these parties maintain armed militias accountable to the party leaders. And the leaders of virtually all these parties—or their predecessors, since many of the parties emerged in their current form only after the US occupation—spent their years of exile during Saddam Hussein's rule in Iran. Many married Iranians, and mixed Iraqi–Iranian families are common. There is $2 billion worth of annual trade between the two countries even with Iraq under US occupation. It is no wonder that so many Iraqis have ties to Iran. The two countries' history is as much a history of linkage and connection as it is of competition and nationalist rivalry.

Competition among regional powers in the Middle East is an old story; Iran and Iraq, the two countries with oil wealth, water, and large population and territory, were long-time rivals for regional dominance. The neighboring Arab countries sided with Iraq in that contest, supporting Iraq during the Iran–Iraq war and continuing to see Iran as a regional threat even after the 2003 overthrow of Iraq's government and the consolidation of the US-led occupation. So, ironically, some of the antagonism toward the US occupation-backed Iraqi government by neighboring Arab regimes reflects unease about Baghdad's ties with Iran. Not particularly because Iran is Shi'a and the Arab states largely Sunni, but because Iran is a traditional competitor and without Iraq, long the most powerful Arab country, to provide a buffer, the Arab governments fear Iran's regional power. At the same time, many of the Arab governments face huge problems at home, where their populations are overwhelmingly opposed to the US occupation of Iraq; while none of the Arab regimes are particularly concerned about public opinion, they all recognize that domestic anger at the sight of Arab leaders embracing the occupation-backed leader of Iraq could threaten instability and potentially even inspire a challenge to their power.

As for Turkey, its concern with Iraq is almost all about the Kurds (see "What is the special relationship between Iraqi Kurds and the US?"). Turkey is concerned that the autonomous Kurdish region in northern Iraq is providing a refuge for Kurdish militants who continue to challenge Turkish rule in its own Kurdish region. Turkey has engaged in military attacks, ostensibly against PKK guerrillas but with civilian casualties as well, inside Iraqi territory. The US, which supports the Kurdish regional government in northern Iraq, and of course also has a close strategic relationship with NATO member Turkey, has urged Turkey to use caution in attacking inside Iraqi territory; but Washington has made clear that it wants the Kurdish government to get rid of the PKK camps. On the other hand, in 2007 and 2008, reports surfaced about another Kurdish organization linked to the PKK—this one called PJAK (Party for Free Life in Kurdistan). PJAK is made up of Iranian Kurds whose members attack Iran rather than Turkey, but who are also based in the Kurdish region of Iraq. Israel supports PJAK's anti-Iran mobilization. The complication is that the US supports PJAK attacks on Iran, even while it condemns identical PKK attacks on Turkey.[119] So the role of Turkey in Iraq remains volatile. Turkey's primary goal is to ensure that the Kurdish region of Iraq does not break away into an independent state, providing a model and perhaps a refuge for anti-Turkish Kurdish militants. The resulting instability and uncertainty that exist under conditions of occupation are not likely to change qualitatively in a post-occupation environment.

Lastly, Iran has made clear its eagerness to make sure Iraq's instability does not spill over its border. Tehran has established closer diplomatic ties and economic relations with the occupation-backed Iraqi government than any other country in the region has. Washington's opposition to Iran has of course challenged that relationship, particularly its many provocative actions, such as arresting Iranian diplomats who are in Iraq at the invitation of the Iraqi government, identifying Iran as the primary source of instability in Iraq and the basis for why the US occupation must remain, and building a huge new military base less than five miles from the Iranian border. Without those provocations, relations between Iran and Iraq would have a much better chance at normalization.

What can the US Congress do about the war?

Congress essentially abdicated its constitutional responsibility to declare or reject war in 2002 when it gave the Bush administration the power to decide whether to go to war against Iraq. So the US invasion of 2003 and the long years of war and occupation since have all been waged without a declaration of war.

But Congress still bears ultimate power—the power to approve or deny the use of funds to pay for the war. Despite almost eight years of Bush administration efforts to consolidate governmental power in the executive branch, Congress still controls the purse strings of the US budget. From the first years of the war, many members of Congress, most but not all of them Democrats, declared their opposition to the Iraq war and their intention to stop funding it. But they never made good on that intention. For the first three years of the war, Congress maintained a Republican majority that largely supported the war. But even after the November 2006 elections that brought a Democratic majority to both houses of Congress with a clear antiwar mandate, Congress continued to provide the Bush administration with every penny it asked for to continue funding the war.

The administration's strategy, maintained throughout the years of war and occupation, was to keep the funding requests for Iraq (and Afghanistan) separate from the regular annual budget appropriation debates. The escalating "regular" military budget reached $504 billion by FY 2008—more than half a *trillion* dollars. And that did not include the hundreds of billions of dollars appropriated each year for the wars in Iraq and Afghanistan. Those appropriations were requested in separate supplemental funding bills—a method generally intended for emergency or unexpected costs, not the relentless anticipated costs of a years-long war. The advantage to the White House is that the supplemental funding bills are not subject to the same level of scrutiny as the regular budget.

Many in the 72-member Progressive Caucus, the newer Out of Iraq Caucus, and the Congressional Black Caucus tried various strategies to impose conditions on the supplemental funding bills, but none of their efforts did anything to slow the war's brutal trajectory. They got bills passed prohibiting the construction of "permanent bases" in Iraq, but the construction of the giant, town-sized military bases continued, because in the Pentagon's parlance they weren't "permanent bases" but "enduring bases." Progressive Caucus and Out of Iraq Caucus leaders Barbara Lee, Lynn Woolsey, and Maxine Waters crafted a bill that would prohibit any funding for the Iraq war except to bring home the troops—knowing that if it ever won enough votes to pass, it would certainly be vetoed by the president. But it never passed. And even though the Democrats controlled both houses of Congress, their congressional leadership continued to use the excuse that they did not have the votes to overturn Bush's certain veto of any conditions on war funding, as a way of explaining their failure to end the war.

In fact the Democrats' "we don't have the votes" claim was true—but also irrelevant. Overturning a presidential veto wasn't necessary. All Congress had to do was to refuse to vote each supplemental war funding bill out of committee, refuse to send it to the floor of the House for a vote. With no floor vote, there would be no bill for the president to veto—and there would be no further funding for the war. The troops would have to be brought home.

But Congress remained afraid, and the fear paralyzed all but the most committed members. They were not afraid of what would happen in Iraq; they were not afraid of consequences on the battlefield— but they were very afraid of the political reper- cussions. The fear was not about what would happen to the soldiers, who would finally have to be brought home—the fear was about the headline the day after the vote, saying "Democrats Abandon the Troops." It wasn't abandonment, of course, it was the most profound kind of support for the safety of the troops, to bring them safely home. But the political fear overcame all else—and Congress refused to use the one clear method at their disposal to stop the funding.

By the spring of 2008, only months remained in the Bush administration and a new $168 billion supplemental budget request for the Iraq and Afghanistan wars was looming. In that same period, the Democratic-controlled Congress had used the "don't vote it out of committee" tactic to stop two important (but not Iraq war–related) Bush priorities. As the *Washington Post* described it:

> After years of seeing the House pushed around by President Bush, Speaker Nancy Pelosi has learned to say no. The California Democrat's refusal last month to schedule a vote on a warrantless surveillance bill that the president favors, followed by her decision this month to scuttle a fast-track vote on a US–Colombia trade agreement have shifted some power to the eastern end of Pennsylvania Avenue [Congress]. But those tough stands also have raised expectations among antiwar activists and some lawmakers on the larger issue coming in the next two weeks: funding for the war in Iraq. "What she's done is show people you can stand up to Bush and it's not the end of the world," said Rep. Jim McGovern (D-Mass.), a prominent opponent of the Iraq war. "She reminded the rank-and-file here not only do we matter, but we're an equal branch of government, and she reminded the president we're no longer a cheap date."[120]

As the *Post* continued, "For many Democrats, the standoffs on terrorist surveillance and the Colombia trade deal have been eye-opening for their lack of political fallout." Congress said no to the Bush administration and lived to tell the tale. The real question would come a few weeks later, when Congress faced the latest demand for more unconditional funding of the war they had so long claimed to oppose, even while paying every dime.

The model used to stop the Colombia free trade agreement and warrantless surveillance could have been the most powerful instrument Congress has to end the war—by stopping funding for the war. But it didn't happen. The Democrats blinked. On July 19, 2008, the latest supplemental funding bill was passed, signed into law on July 30. The Democratic members of Congress who had supported the bill tried to convince their angry constituents that it was all okay because the bill included increased funding for veterans' education opportunities. But the bottom line was that, despite the antiwar majority, Congress enabled the war and occupation of Iraq to continue.

Are opponents of the war really soft on terrorism?

The Iraq war is not making Americans—let alone Iraqis or anyone else in the world—safer from terrorist attacks. As early as the first year of the war, the International Institute for Strategic Studies in London had determined that the Iraq war had "actually strengthened the al Qaeda terrorist network, rather than weakening it." It said that the occupation of Iraq had become al-Qaeda's most "potent global recruitment pretext" and had "led to an accelerated recruitment to Al-Qaeda."[121]

Many in the US point to the claim that the war in Iraq is also a "distraction" from what is viewed as the more appropriate or more legitimate war in Afghanistan. As noted above (see "Isn't the Iraq war distracting the US from the real war against terrorism in Afghanistan?") the US attack on Afghanistan was illegal and didn't qualify as self-defense. Certainly the Afghanistan–Pakistan border area appears to be a gathering point for al-Qaeda and perhaps other terror organizations. But war and occupation *have not*, most likely *cannot*, and almost certainly *will not* end terrorism. Terrorism means an attack on civilians designed to send a political message—and terrorism can be carried out by suicide bomb or by F-16 attack, by secret cells or by powerful armies. Terrorism is a tool, an instrument, not a strategy. The types of attack most commonly identified as terrorism, such as suicide bombings, are chosen by those—within or outside of govern-ments—willing to use illegal violence against civilians but lacking the F-16 fighter jets, Apache helicopters, and other weapons used by wealthier, more powerful forces also prepared to attack civilians.

From its origins, the specific terrorism of al-Qaeda had very specific goals: to force the Saudi Arabian government to expel the US "infidels" from what was considered to be holy ground. When the secular—thus also "infidel"—Saddam Hussein's forces invaded Kuwait in 1990, Osama bin Laden offered the Saudis 100,000 Muslim warriors to repel the invaders, to avoid the humiliation and religious outrage of having US or other Western troops in the region. The Saudis rejected his offer. And in the almost two decades since, more US troops were stationed in the region, culminating in what appears to be a permanent US occupation of Iraq involving hundreds of thousands of soldiers and mercenaries. Should anyone be surprised that terrorist attacks increased as well?

A serious effort to stop terrorism must look seriously at its causes. It is unlikely that, after so many years of building anger and hostility, even a significant shift in US or UK policy in the Middle East will eliminate all threats of terrorist attack; certainly there are extremist elements bent on destroying lives for religious, ideological, or other reasons. But there is little doubt that the vast majority of participants in terrorist activities, many of them angered and motivated by the US occupation of Iraq, US support for Israeli occupation of Palestinian land, and US backing of corrupt dictatorships across the Middle East would view the world very differently if those policies were reversed. Osama bin Laden was a longstanding CIA asset throughout the years of the anti-Soviet *mujahideen* struggle in Afghanistan in the 1980s, and it is unlikely that he will change his anti-American views based on anything the US might do today. But there is every reason to believe that a serious change in US policies—policies so often in violation of international and often even US domestic laws—would change the views of many around the world who otherwise might see Osama bin Laden or al-Qaeda as legitimate, even heroic. And if those potential supporters turn into might-have-been-but-aren't, wouldn't we all be safer?

Invading and occupying Iraq is helping to foment, not to end, terrorism. A real effort to stop global terrorism requires real collaboration, real cooperation, real multilateralism, real respect for international law and the United Nations, and real support for international institutions such as the International Criminal Court. The terrorist attacks of September 11, 2001, were a terrible crime against humanity in which almost 3,000 people were killed. On September 12, 2001, and on every day since, another terrible crime against humanity has been committed, resulting each day in more than 36,000 children around the world being killed by preventable hunger and preventable disease. If the billions of dollars—more than $3 trillion dollars in the longer term—of US tax money that has gone to pay for the war in Iraq had instead been used to end world hunger; to provide every child in the developing world with immunizations, clean water, and education; and to create environmentally sustainable agriculture and industry for a growing global population, then the threat of terrorism would be dramatically decreased. Instead the US government is presiding over a world in which the three wealthiest individuals in the world are worth more than the GNP of the 48 poorest countries in the world.

Terrorism isn't necessarily committed by the poorest of the poor, but poverty breeds disempowerment and hopelessness, and national disempowerment and hopelessness breeds humiliation even in those who do not directly experience it. US and earlier UK economic, military, corporate, and cultural policies have all played a role in creating those conditions in countries in the Middle East and around the world. War in Iraq only exacerbates that reality.

Instead of responding to September 11 with the threat that "you're either with us, or with the terrorists," and moving to wage war and assert control of people and nations across the globe, the US answer to terrorism should have begun with international law. The US should have embraced the International Criminal Court they had so long demonized, but instead on May 6, 2002, the Bush administration formally renounced the treaty President Bill Clinton had so grudgingly signed. Bush officials said the new court should expect no cooperation from the United States, and that Washington would not provide ICC prosecutors with any information that might help them bring cases against any accused war criminals. Then US Ambassador for War Crimes Pierre-Richard Prosper said he could not envision any future situation in which the US would assist the court. "We've washed our hands. It's over," he said. In May 2002, almost a year before ordering the invasion of Iraq, Secretary of Defense Rumsfeld said that the ICC would "necessarily complicate US military cooperation," looking ahead to his goal of a "coalition of the willing" in Iraq. Given the crimes that were soon to surface in Abu Ghraib, Guantánamo and elsewhere, it was particularly ironic that Rumsfeld added that an international court with jurisdiction over genocide, war crimes, and crimes against humanity "could well create a powerful disincentive for US military engagement in the world."[122]

But a central role for the International Criminal Court and indeed international justice against terrorism was denied in Afghanistan and denied in Iraq. The global cooperation envisioned by the International Criminal Court was rejected, and instead a coalition of coercion based on US unilateral power backed by an acquiescent UK government was the only option offered. War was the only answer offered in response to terrorism. That has not made anyone safer.

What will happen if the US and UK end the occupation, withdraw all their troops, and close the military bases?

No one knows exactly what will happen when the US-led troops pull out; anyone who claims they *know* is lying. It is possible, though, to anticipate the most likely scenarios and consequences, based on what we know of past and current situations on the ground and who the players are.

Unfortunately, it is quite likely that the first reaction to the pullout of US, British, other "coalition," and mercenary troops will be a spurt of escalated violence, as various forces in Iraq jockey for power. But probably such an escalation of violence will be of very short duration—a matter of weeks, not months. The longer-term and more significant response will almost certainly happen as Iraqis recognize that the occupation is at last ending. At that point, those resistance groups whose target has been the US–UK occupation forces will largely stop fighting and stand down altogether, since their raison d'être will have disappeared. The violence of occupation and anti-occupation resistance will come to an end.

That does not mean all violence will stop, however. Many of those militant groups that have targeted Iraqi civilians in terror attacks—motivated by power, money, sectarian interests, religious, or other extremist ideologies—have also targeted the occupation troops. While those forces whose *only* target is the occupation will likely stop fighting, those who also want to transform Iraqi society into their own version of an ethnically or religiously "pure" state will likely continue their violence. However, it should not be forgotten that 61 percent of Iraqis tell pollsters that they support attacks on US troops—while only 7 percent say they support attacks on other Iraqis. That means that what will likely begin to change very quickly is the current reluctance, even refusal, of many Iraqis to challenge those terrorist forces attacking civilians because they are *also* targeting US occupation troops. And once ordinary Iraqis— including those participating in the anti-occupation resistance—begin to identify and isolate those terrorist forces, they can begin what is currently impossible: eliminating the terrorists as fighting forces and as threats to Iraqi society.

The reduction and probably rapid elimination of occupation-driven terrorism and other violence in Iraq does not, of course, mean the complete demilitarization and de-weaponization of Iraqi society as a whole. The armed militias that play such a major role in Iraqi life under occupation will likely continue—even now, many of them have their origins in political/social welfare organizations operating within particular ethnic, religious, or other communities within Iraq; the armed militias emerged as political and power struggles in occupied Iraq took an increasingly violent form.

But soon after the US-led occupying armies leave Iraq, the overall level of violence will most likely be reduced. One example can be seen in Basra, the oil-rich, largely Shi'a city in southern Iraq that had been occupied by British troops since 2003. When the British forces were withdrawn from most of the city, attacks dropped by 90 percent. As the British General Graham Binns told reporters in November 2007, "We thought, if 90 percent of the violence is directed at us, what would happen if we stepped back?" Analyzing the impact of the 5,000 British troops moving out of the heart of Basra in September, Binns said there had been "a remarkable and dramatic drop in attacks. The motivation for attacking us was gone, because we're no longer patrolling the streets." British officials said they expected a spike in what they called "intra-militia violence" after their troops pulled back, but were surprised to find none.[123] Certainly the violence in Basra had not completely ended; there was a temporary week-long spike in fighting in spring 2008 in response to a US-backed Iraqi government military attack on the dominant Shi'a militia in Basra. But there is no question that the withdrawal of occupation troops led to a massive reduction in overall violence.

There is every reason to believe that the withdrawal of *all* US and British occupying troops, other "coalition" forces, and all the US-paid non-Iraqi mercenaries will further the goal of reducing violence and allowing Iraqis to reclaim their country. There is certainly a good possibility that the current govern-ment may not survive an end to the occupation that created it and has kept it in power these last several years. That harsh reality reflects the fact that Prime Minister Maliki's government has not managed to maintain the level of domestic credibility and legitimacy that would allow it to remain in power as a truly independent, sovereign government relying for support on the willing consent of the governed. Even the apparent incremental rise in Maliki's credibility as "surge" troops were withdrawn in mid-

2008 does not mean his US-backed government would survive a full US withdrawal. Exactly what political forces would emerge to fill a post-occupation partial or total vacuum remains uncertain; but it's likely that national figures, most though not all emerging out of religious power bases, would compete for power. The degree to which that power struggle would remain nonviolent and political rather than military depends a great deal on the ability of Iraqi civil society, secular as well as religious, to survive the ravages of the US occupation.

It is certainly true that Iraqis voting in the 2005 elections showed an extraordinary level of public craving for democracy, an amazing eagerness to participate, and incredible courage in taking the risk of voting in the face of serious threats. However, as is the case in so many countries around the world, the elections did not bring democracy, real representation, or empowerment of the Iraqi population. The elected parties—mostly sectarian parties created by or empowered with US acquiescence and assistance to represent specific religious or ethnic communities—won seats based on campaign promises that they would ask the US to end the occupation. But once in power, many of those elected realized they were dependent on the US to keep them in the (relative) privilege and security of the Iraqi parliament, and they reneged on their campaign promises. The cabinet grew more and more unaccountable even to the parliament, let alone to the Iraqi people, and tensions continue to rise between the executive and legislative branches. Thus, despite the fact that 80 percent or more Iraqis want the occupation to end and all foreign troops to be withdrawn, and despite a spring 2007 parliamentary resolution that called for a timetable for such withdrawal, in the fall of 2007, the Maliki government, backed by the US, succeeded in persuading the United Nations Security Council to extend its mandate authorizing the so-called multinational force, the US-led occupying army, to remain in Iraq until December 31, 2008. By summer 2008, while neither President Bush nor Prime Minister Maliki were serious about wanting to withdraw US troops from Iraq, both were under rising election-driven pressure to support some kind of timetable for withdrawal. They quickly agreed on a call to set a "time horizon." It was a sound-bite dodge, not a commitment to end the occupation. Few missed the harsh reality that the most important characteristic of a "horizon" is that while it may look nice from a distance, you can never actually get there.

Again, no one can absolutely guarantee what will happen when the US and UK occupation troops leave Iraq. But we do know with certainty what will happen if they do *not* withdraw: the occupation troops will continue to kill and continue to die, the contractor-driven "reconstruction" process will remain stalled, the Iraqi "government" will remain illegitimate in the minds of the Iraqi people, and the overall situation in the country will remain dire.

The withdrawal of US and UK occupation troops will not, by itself, end all the violence and turn Iraq into a Switzerland of the Middle East. Iraqis themselves still face an almost incomprehensibly difficult struggle to reclaim, rebuild, and reunify their country. But *until* the withdrawal of occupation troops takes place, there is no chance for Iraqis to even begin that long challenge.

If 70 percent of Americans want to end the war, why is it continuing?

The US antiwar movement that cohered in the fall of 2002, even before plans for the invasion of Iraq were officially made public, set a clear goal for itself: to transform public opinion from what was then only 22 percent opposition to the war to an overwhelming majority. It seemed a daunting task. But within the first few years of the war and occupation, the goal of an opposition majority had been achieved. Certainly the work of the antiwar movement was not the only reason for the dramatic change in public opinion; increasing recognition that the US was losing the war in Iraq and the rising number of US casualties played a huge role. (Though it must be acknowledged that the truly horrific—but publicly largely unknown and unacknowledged—toll of Iraqi civilians killed in the war did not appear to play a significant role in changing US public opinion.)

There has been a similarly consistent rise in antiwar opinion in the UK during this time. As was true in Spain and Italy, also early governmental supporters of the Iraq invasion, the UK's enthusiastic support for the war and occupation of Iraq never matched public opinion. Antiwar organizations continued major mobilization, and antiwar sentiment continued to rise. Unlike their Spanish and Italian counterparts, British antiwar campaigners did not see a shift away from the pro-war party when Prime Minister Tony Blair was replaced by Gordon Brown in 2007. Instead, the defeat of Tony Blair was within an internal Labor Party battle, and he was simply replaced by his long-time junior partner. But Brown, while rhetorically cautious in distancing himself from the Iraq war and George Bush, allowed a significant (though not total) troop withdrawal within the first year of his premiership. The redeployment of British troops out of the center of Basra in August–September 2007 set the stage for a July 2008 announcement hinting at a much fuller withdrawal by summer 2009. But the work of Britain's antiwar movement remains crucial to holding a reluctant Brown to his commitments.

The challenge facing US opponents of the war emerged more sharply toward the end of 2004 and early 2005, when majority opposition had been achieved. While opposition continued to rise (reaching about 70 percent in the US by early 2008), the realization emerged that public opinion was not a driving force in determining US policy toward Iraq. This was an administration, and a Congress, that had no intention of ending the most unpopular war in history simply because the American people, the Iraqi people, and most of the world wanted to end it. President Bush dismissed massive public opposition as a "focus group." Vice President Cheney, when reminded of the two-thirds of Americans who opposed the war, sneeringly answered, "so?"[124] Congressional Democrats remained so frightened of headlines blaming them for "abandoning the troops" that they refused to cut war funding, and instead handed the White House every billion dollars it requested.

No antiwar movement in the United States had ever achieved such success in changing public opinion, and no antiwar movement in the United States had ever faced a government less accountable to public opinion. The post-9/11 pall of fear that had paralyzed so many people, and had been so successfully renewed over and over again by the White House in the interest of mobilizing support for war, was finally ebbing by 2007 and 2008. But the fear remained powerful inside Washington, and it was matched in Congress by a political fear of being accused of being "soft on security."

The military's own capacity was certainly already stretched by the repeated long deployments. The "stop-loss" law that allowed the Pentagon to redeploy US troops even when their contractually agreed term in the military was over was used to great effect to keep the numbers high, but had a terrible impact on the health and morale of the soldiers, as well as on their families. Active-duty soldiers were joining antiwar military families and veterans in building resistance to the war within the military institutions. Recruitment was indeed dropping, but the Pentagon responded by lowering the criteria for new soldiers. The military accepted more recruits who lacked high school diplomas, and increased the quota for convicted criminals. In 2006 alone, the US Army enlisted 8,129 felons, including those convicted of aggravated assault, burglary, and robbery based on "moral waivers."[125]

The recession that hit so hard in 2007–2008 brought the economic costs of the war to new prominence in public discourse, but voices in Washington continued the official line that the war had nothing to do with the overall economic crisis. Tax cuts for corporations and the richest Americans remained in place, and the costs of the war continued to be paid for on credit—with the bill to be paid by future generations. The online antiwar organization MoveOn.org, following a set of surveys in April 2008 that indicated that a large majority of Americans believed that war spending was a major cause of the economic crisis, urged that the money being spent on the Iraq war instead be used for domestic needs[126]—but the voices of those overwhelming antiwar majorities were largely ignored. War spending continued and the economic crisis deepened.

Several years into the war, the mainstream media, including the *New York Times*, the *Washington Post*, and others, began a series of sometimes serious (however late in coming) mea culpas for the role they had played in uncritically accepting Bush administration lies about WMDs, links between Iraq and al-Qaeda, and more, as well as their overall cheerleading for the war in its early stages. But the press largely failed to reverse course and still failed to hold politicians (of *either* party) accountable for their continuing support for the war, demand serious answers to serious questions, or engage in sufficient independent investigations. While critical exposés were published (on Cheney's role in war-making decisions, on deplorable conditions facing wounded soldiers in Walter Reed Army Hospital, and much more), they were notable as much for being rare as for being important. And each time the rhetoric against Iran escalated, in 2006, 2007, and again in 2008, the mainstream media in the US overwhelmingly fell into line, parroting statements from the White House, segueing from allegation to fact, and helping build support for the possibility of an even more reckless war.

So it turned out the work of changing opinion hasn't been enough. The other pillars of support for the Iraq war and occupation—congressional/political support, military capacity, financing, media support/acquiescence—have largely remained intact, and the war continues.

What will it take to force the US government to end the war?

The Bush administration has shown itself to be reckless and dangerous, willing to launch and continue an illegal war in defiance of the United Nations, in violation of the US Constitution, and in opposition to majority public opinion. Throughout the years of the Iraq war, Congress, with far too few exceptions, has shown itself to be too weak and concerned with political consequences to take responsibility for the disastrous consequences the war has brought to Iraqis and Americans alike, and too afraid to deny the president funding to continue the war. The mainstream media has shown itself to be incapable of the kind of sustained, critical examination that would help discredit and delegitimize the war policies. And while all of these efforts are required to challenge the war policies of the UK, it is clear that Washington, not London, is calling the shots in Iraq, and that a qualitative reversal of the US war posture would allow for a quick turnabout in the UK as well.

Into the Streets

So what can people who live in the US do to change the situation? Certainly the work of demonstrating the size and power of antiwar opinion across the country remains crucial. National and nationally coordinated regional and local protests and demonstrations, such as those organized by the huge

United for Peace and Justice coalition, must continue. Those mobilizations can be strengthened and built on by linking their organizing to petition drives and campaigns aimed at reaching local, municipal, and state as well as national officials, and following them with teach-ins, lobby days, and other related actions. To demonstrate strength, rather than showing weakness, big protests requires not only size, but breadth, diversity, and centrality. That is, we need not only lots of people participating, but each demonstration needs to show the range of people— crossing race, age, gender, nationality, class, sexual orientation, immigration and military status, language, and other lines—who oppose the war. We need to showcase the wide range of communities affected by the war—and the resulting multiplicity of reasons people oppose the war.

Congress

Continuing pressure on Congress will be necessary as long as the war continues. With only a few exceptions, Congress, despite its Democratic majority, remains partisan, weak, and frightened. The moment Congress perceives that the political cost of funding the war has risen above the cost of ending the war, they will do what has become politically expedient. The pressure must take many forms and involve combined "inside/outside" strategies—from phone-in days and letter-writing drives from constituents, to demands that members of Congress participate in open discussions and town hall meetings and debates on the war, to working with congressional and committee staff on potential legislation, to mobilizing protests outside members' headquarters in their districts or their Capitol offices in Washington, DC.

Education

Education must continue to have pride of place among all those trying to end the war. Conviction and moral outrage alone will not be enough to convince those who don't agree with us and to empower our own supporters to move beyond their comfort zones to reach broader audiences. We continue to need clear and concise information to counter those who argue "we can't cut and run," or "we have to stay to support the troops," or "we have to stay because there will be chaos if we leave" or "we have to fight them there so we don't have to fight them here" or "we have to win the war because they hate us." Books and pamphlets, television and radio shows, online and interactive discussions, video and other new media tools, and much more must all be utilized. Teach-ins, classes and discussions at high schools and universities, publication in mainstream and progressive media outlets, book groups and discussions, claiming public spaces such as libraries for new kinds of interactive events—all must be part of the antiwar arsenal.

Iraqi Victims, Iraqi Voices

Education in this context also means learning from Iraqi voices, and keeping Iraq and Iraqis central to any discussion of the costs of war. With official State Department polls indicating that eight out of ten Iraqis oppose the US–UK occupation, the voices of those anti-occupation Iraqis remain a critical, though far too often ignored, component of the global and US antiwar movement. Some in the antiwar movement have consistently focused on the devastation the war has brought to Iraq and its people. The American Friends Service Committee, the Nobel peace laureate organization of Quaker activism, created an exhibition early in the occupation that featured rows of military boots, each pair labeled with the name of a US soldier killed in Iraq or Afghanistan. The rows expanded as the US casualty levels rose. But soon it became clear to AFSC that demonstrating the cost to Iraqis was equally if not more important, and they responded by adding to the exhibit a huge pile of unlabeled shoes—baby shoes, children's play shoes, teenagers' soccer shoes and sneakers, adults' shoes of every sort, grandma-style shoes, all reminding viewers of just who is living—and dying—under the violence of the US war and occupation of Iraq.

The labor movement–based US Labor Against the War organized an extraordinary exchange of workers, with US trade union activists traveling to occupied Iraq to meet with Iraqi workers, while a delegation of Iraqi oil workers' union federations toured the United

States, meeting with antiwar activists, trade unionists, church and student groups, and many others. Internationally, engagement with Iraqi activists has become a regular component of the work of global social movements. In one example, a consortium of Italian, British, Filipino, Dutch, US, and other activists came together at the Transnational Institute in Amsterdam to collaborate on plans for ongoing engagement with Iraqi civil-society organizations.

Broader Coalitions, Strange Bedfellows

It's a given that forcing a reluctant and recalcitrant government to end this disastrous war will not be easy. It will require the mobilization of and unity-building efforts among constituencies far beyond the already committed and self-defined antiwar movement. It will mean rigorous analysis of how the costs of this war—the human, financial, environmental, social, and other costs—affect communities across the United States. The African-American community has seen a huge drop in military recruitment levels, but still makes up a disproportionate number of recruits, and that means more than its share of casualties; it is already deeply antiwar and should be recognized as a far more visible central component of the antiwar movement. Latino enlistment now accounts for more than a quarter of all new recruits—and with job and education options diminishing, that can be expected to rise, and offer a clear focus for antiwar mobilization.

New pressures on immigrant communities, including far more restrictions on legalization and citizenship requirements and an overall rise in anti-immigrant repression, leads more young foreign nationals to accept offers of a fast-track to US citizenship if they join the military—an offer too many of them don't live to take advantage of. The immigrant rights activism of the last several years has a clear link to how the so-called war on terrorism has profoundly damaged communities within the US itself.

Rural and small-town residents across the United States represent an overwhelmingly disproportionate number of recruits and casualties—drafted by lack of other opportunities. And students and young people in general are paying a huge price for this war not only in loss of tax money that should go to support education, but also among those who find themselves forced to join the military as the only means of paying for college. The US labor movement, beleaguered as it is in the anti-union 21st century, remains a key center of antiwar views; the May 1, 2008, longshore workers' shutdown of every port on the West Coast, from San Diego to Seattle to protest the Iraq war, was one example. Churches and other faith-based organizations remain stalwart in opposing the war and often can play a key role in pulling together broader coalitions, interfaith gatherings of influential religious leaders in a given community, and influencing local editorial boards, members of Congress, and more, all framed around moral opposition to the war.

For antiwar movements and activists, broadening constituencies also means recognizing how the Iraq war has divided powerful elites across governmental, military, financial, intellectual, and other power centers in the US. There is no elite consensus on the war in Iraq, a reality that makes antiwar mobilization simultaneously more complicated and potentially more powerful. But it necessitates reaching beyond our ordinary comfort zones, to figure out ways of engaging with those far more privileged forces—it means engaging seriously with power. Recognizing and dealing with strange bedfellows does not mean accepting their power-driven, US-centric vantage point, or their generally limited critique of the war. But when Henry Kissinger, Brent Scowcroft, James Baker, and others of their kind oppose military recklessness and urge caution, that's important. When five years into the war even the Pentagon's National Defense University's own National Institute for Strategic Studies says "the war in Iraq has achieved the status of a major war and a major debacle,"[127] those opinions matter and should be used to strengthen the peace movement's own influence and legitimacy.

The Kissingers of the world and the Pentagon's strategic analysts were late coming to this recognition—the American and British people, not to mention those in Iraq, understood the folly and the horror of this war long before them. But however late, it is still a good thing that eventually even longtime war supporters are recognizing this particular war's failure. And peace activists should recognize and celebrate how the elites' willingness to do so publicly rather than in secret has everything to do with the antiwar movement's success in transforming public opinion so that asserting an antiwar position no longer carries political risk.

Inside / Outside

Engaging with power requires a more complex web of what we might call inside/outside strategies. Some of those working to end the war need to be inside, in the room, working with members of Congress or other officials who might be trying to reduce the damage done by one particular war policy, such as by limiting spending on specific aspects of the war or opposing construction of new permanent bases in Iraq. Others, by far most of the war's opponents and peace activists, will remain outside the room, asserting their full principle of demanding a *real* end to the war—demanding that those in power bring home *all* the troops, repatriate *all* the foreign mercenaries, close down all the *existing* as well as planned US military bases in Iraq, end *all* efforts to control Iraqi oil.

It is unlikely we can fully end the war all at once. So it should not be seen as a failure if an incremental step leads "only" to somehow improving the lives of Iraqis suffering under occupation, even if that particular step did not end the war. If, for example, an effort to completely prevent Congress from passing a new funding bill fails, it is still better if the bill finally passed authorizes only $1 billion rather than $100 billion. It is never a victory as long as the war itself continues, but that kind of limited result can still, to some degree, restrict the options available to those commanding the war and spending the war funds, and it keeps the issue on the public agenda so we can return to fight again.

The danger is not in winning only partial advances, or achieving only partial gains. The danger lies in settling for what is possible at a given moment, instead of continuing to fight for what is truly necessary: ending the war. Completely. This danger emerges when antiwar forces become so focused on a specific, limited possibility of influencing how the war is waged that they abandon their real convictions regarding what really ending the war requires.

Within the intersecting inside and outside strategies, different organizations and movements— or sometimes different people within the same organization, or once in a while even the same person—will play different but collaborative roles, moving from off-the-record congressional staff meetings to street protests where the focus remains *ending* the war, not simply reducing its harm.

Alternative Centers of Power
However sophisticated our understanding of inside/outside strategies and the need to influence Congress in many different ways, one of the clearest

lessons of the Bush years has been that Congress has been unwilling and therefore unable to rein in the extremism and recklessness of this administration. That means that antiwar forces must broaden our definitions of where influence lies, expanding what it means to engage with power.

The Cities for Peace movement, which began at the Institute for Policy Studies in the fall of 2002, many months before the invasion of Iraq, provides one such example. Before the invasion, local organizing focused on mobilizing support for city council resolutions or mayors' proclamations opposing the war; throughout the years of occupation the resolutions demanded that US troops be brought home. Soon after the initiative began at the municipal level, similar peace drives took shape in numerous counties and even states. Many of the resolutions focused on the illegality of the war, some honed in on why local National Guard or reserve troops should be brought home, almost all expressed outrage at how local resources—financial, human, first-responder capacity, and more—were being squandered on an illegal and/or unnecessary and/or failing war.

In early June 2005, the governor of Montana, hardly a hotbed of antiwar sentiment but facing an unusually dangerous wildfire season, asked the Pentagon, "Why don't you send Montana's Guardsmen home for July and August?" The commander of the Montana Guard had described an "unprecedented" shortage of both firefighters deployed in Iraq and

Montana's helicopters, ten out of twelve of which were also stuck in Iraq and unavailable for fighting fires. As the *Boston Globe* noted dryly, "The Pentagon has refused his request." The *Globe* also recognized that Montana Governor Brian Schweitzer had "tapped a sense of anxiety among governors whose troops are fighting the insurgency in Iraq with no end in sight."[129]

The Cities for Peace movement was based on the idea that, facing a weak and vacillating Congress, it was necessary to find and mobilize antiwar opinion within alternative centers of power, with the goal of broadening and deepening the existing public delegitimation of the Iraq war. That process could help raise the political cost of supporting the war, and thus help strengthen congressional, and other, opposition. By 2008 more than 286 cities, 19 counties, and 17 entire states had passed resolutions calling on the Bush administration to bring the troops home.[130] Together, those Cities, Counties, and States for Peace represented more than 50 percent of the US population.

The Costs of War
The local/municipal/state-based organizing has two major strengths. First, working at the local level allows greater engagement with civic life than is often the case in challenging national policies. Second, it provides an immediate link to the costs of war at a scale and in language that everyone could understand. The concept of the war costing $3 trillion is such an

abstraction that few can fathom the real meaning. But everyone can grasp the reality that their town, their state, was paying X amount of tax money for the war, and that those funds *could* have been used instead to provide health insurance for X number of children, or to build X number of low-cost housing units, or to hire X number of new teachers for impoverished schools.

The work of organizations like the National Priorities Project (www.nationalpriorities.org) continues to play an enormously important role in providing the antiwar movement with concrete information in a form specifically designed to challenge the war's supporters. The NPP breaks down the seemingly mind-numbing numbers of the federal budget into comparisons—how much for war, how much for education; how much for war in this town, or this state, or this congressional district vs. how much for health care. Similarly, the 2008 campaign launched by the online antiwar mobilization MoveOn.org, which linked the cost of the Iraq war with the escalating recession, provided an important framework for keeping the war and its costs central to public and campaign-based discourse in a period of extreme economic anxiety.

Weakening the War Machine
In addition to the rising public recognition of the human and economic of the Iraq war, growing resistance within and around the military itself has emerged as a key component of antiwar organizing.

The work of counter-recruitment campaigns, aimed at depriving the military of the man- and woman-power needed to actually wage war, remains crucial. The National Priorities Project, beyond their work on the war budget, was also the first organization to document the class basis of military recruiting—tracking the income levels, town populations, and other factors showing which high schools are prioritized and which are bypassed by military recruiters. Iraq Veterans Against the War have shaped their own "truth in recruiting" campaign. Part of their effort focuses on publicizing the little-known "stop-loss" law (see "Didn't the US troops in Iraq all volunteer to be there?").

And beyond the anti-recruitment drives, the growing level of resistance *within* the armed services has, years into the occupation of Iraq, emerged as a major center of antiwar attention and a major concern for the Pentagon. The "Winter Soldier—Iraq and Afghanistan" hearing sponsored by Iraq Veterans Against the War in February 2008, and repeated on Capitol Hill in May, brought the reality of the Iraq war to hundreds of thousands, perhaps millions, of people who watched the live webcast, listened to radio coverage, read the transcripts, or saw clips on television. The hearings documented, through searing testimony of the veterans themselves, how US military officers used derogatory, racist terms for Iraqis in order to dehumanize them in the eyes of their troops; how public claims about "protecting Iraqi civilians" were ignored in the theater of war; how the official "rules of engagement" allowed, even required, actions against civilians that clearly violated international law; how civilian killings were ordered to be covered up, and far more.

Just as the increasing visibility of antiwar veterans returning from Vietnam—including the first Winter Soldier hearings, held in 1970—transformed the breadth and legitimacy of antiwar public opinion, the growing size and public profile of organizations like Iraq Veterans Against the War is strengthening the antiwar movement with a powerful authenticity and authority. As the antiwar movement reaches further to support the growing active-duty military resistance, the role of the antiwar veterans will remain central.

Coming Together

The broad US, UK, and global movements against the war and occupation of Iraq encompass a wide range of organizations, coalitions, campaigns. Women's organizations, civil rights and civil liberties groups, religious constituencies, gay and lesbian mobilizations, trade unions, active-duty military, veterans and their families, African-American, Latino, Arab and Muslim communities, movements fighting for living-wage laws and economic justice, environmental organizations, and so many more, all find themselves challenging the Iraq war as a key target—because that war coheres so much of what needs to be confronted in the world, and represents the opposite of so much we are trying to build in the world.

How to decide what is most important? At any given moment, five things, ten things, will be jockeying for the "most important" position, a hundred things will be competing for what must be done now, today. At any given moment, more people will be needed to do them all. No one can do everything. Everyone can do something. Most of us can do more.

It's a huge war. It requires a huge antiwar movement. There's room for all of it.

NOTES

1 Letter to Congressman Jim McDermott from Major General Stephen M. Goldfein, vice director, the Joint Staff, Department of Defense, Washington DC, 23 July 2008. The specific number of US troops who have been deployed to Iraq—separate from those sent to Afghanistan, Kuwait, Saudi Arabia, or elsewhere—was exceptionally difficult to obtain. The Pentagon's public information sources, the Pentagon's congressional liaison office, the Congressional Research Service, and other government sources were all unable to provide this number.

2 "Iraq Poll: 2007," Global Policy Forum <www.globalpolicy.org/security/issues/iraq/resist/2007/09bbciraqipoll.pdf>.

3 Dan Froomkin, "Whose Report Is It Anyway?", WashingtonPost.com, 16 August 2007 <www.washingtonpost.com/wp-dyn/content/blog/2007/08/16/BL2007081601003.html>.

4 Marc Pitzke, "The Show Must Go On," *Spiegel Online International* 11 September 2007 <www.spiegel.de/international/world/0,1518,504993,00.html>.

5 Peter Beaumont and Joanna Walters, "Greenspan Admits Iraq was About Oil, as Deaths Put at 1.2 Million," *Observer* 16 September 2007.

6 UNHCR spokesperson Jennifer Pagonis, press briefing, Palais des Nations, Geneva, 8 April 2008.

7 Jamie Doward, "Refugees Fight Forced Return to Iraq War Zones," *Observer* 13 April 2008.

8 Beth Gardiner, "Iraqi Refugees Receive Cold Greeting in Britain," *International Herald Tribune* 17 May 2007.

9 Associated Press, "U.S. Lets in Fewer Iraqi Refugees, Not More," 2 January 2008.

10 Amit R. Paley, "Most Iraqis Favor Immediate U.S.

Pullout, Polls Show," *Washington Post* 27 September 2006.

11 2007 poll information from "US Surge Has Failed: Iraqi Poll," BBC, 10 September 2007 <news.bbc.co.uk/2/hi/middle_east/ 6983841.stm>. 2008 poll information from "Iraq Poll: 2008," ABC News, BBC, ARD, and NHK <news.bbc.co.uk/2/shared/bsp/ hi/pdfs/14_03_08iraqpollmarch2008.pdf>.

12 "Iraq Poll September 2007: In Graphics," BBC, 10 September 2007 <news.bbc.co.uk/2/hi/middle_east/ 6983027.stm>.

13 "Iraq Poll: 2007," Global Policy Forum <www.globalpolicy.org/security/issues/iraq/resist/2007 /09bbciraqipoll.pdf>.

14 "Kurds at the Crossroads: 1946–1975 False Starts and False Friends," *PBS Frontline/World* May 2003 <www.pbs.org/frontlineworld/stories/iraq203/crossroad s02.html>.

15 Reuters, 8 March 2005.

16 Carl Conetta, "Radical Departure: Towards a Practical Peace in Iraq," Project on Defense Alternatives, 7 July 2004 <www.comw.org/pda/0407br16.html>.

17 Rajiv Chandrasekaran and Walter Pincus, "U.S. Edicts Curb Power Of Iraq's Leadership," *Washington Post* 27 June 2004.

18 Ibid.

19 Naomi Klein, "Bring Halliburton Home," *Nation* 6 November 2003.

20 Tom Nagy, "The Secret Behind the Sanctions: How the U.S. Intentionally Destroyed Iraq's Water Supply," *Progressive*, September 2001.

21 Interview with Leslie Stahl, *Sixty Minutes*, CBS, 12 May 1996.

22 "Choice of Words Matters," BBC News online, 16 September 2004.

23 Müge Gürsöy Sökmen, ed., *World Tribunal on Iraq: Making the Case Against War* (Northampton: Olive Branch Press, 2008).

24 AP, "Geneva Conventions Protect Wounded in War," *USA Today* 16 November 2004.

25 Ibid.

26 Anthony Alessandrini, "The Violation of the Will of the Global Antiwar Movement as a Crime against Peace," in Sökmen, *World Tribunal on Iraq*.

27 Part I Article 1(4) Protocol Additional to the Geneva Conventions of 12 August 1949, and relating to the Protection of Victims of International Armed Conflicts (Protocol 1), 1977.

28 Orly Halpern, "Seeds of Nonviolent Struggle Sown in Iraq," *Christian Science Monitor* 2 June 2004.

29 <www.laonf.net>.

30 <www.unponteper.it/english/ pagina.php?op= include&doc=activity>.

31 Scott Keeter, "Knowledge of Iraq Fatalities Plummets," Pew Research Center for the People and the Press, 12 March 2008 <pewresearch.org/pubs/762/ political-knowledge-update>.

32 Charles W. Hoge, et al., "Combat Duty in Iraq and Afghanistan, Mental Health Problems, and Barriers to Care," *New England Journal of Medicine* 1 July 2004 <content.nejm.org/cgi/content/full/351/1/13>.

33 John Koopman, "30% of Vets Face Stress Disorder, Dr. Says," *San Francisco Chronicle* 4 March 2008 <www.sfgate.com/cgi-bin/article.cgi?f=/c/a/2008/03/ 04/BAEAVD1JI.DTL>.

34 David Barstow, "Behind TV Analysts, Pentagon's Hidden Hand," *New York Times* 20 April 2008.

35 Amy Belasco, "The Cost of Iraq, Afghanistan and Other Global War on Terror Operations Since 9/11," CRS Report for Congress, 8 February 2008.

36 Linda Bilmes and Joseph Stiglitz, *The Three Trillion Dollar War* (New York: W.W. Norton, 2008).

37 David D. Kirkpatrick, "Broad Response to 9/11 Offers Outline of a McCain Doctrine," *New York Times* 17 August 2008.

38 Senator Donald W. Riegle, chairman, Senate Committee on Banking, Housing, and Urban Affairs, "Forward Deployment of Iraqi Chemical Agents During the Persian Gulf War," Senate hearing, 8 October 1994 <www.dsjf.org/Cong%20Hearings/DEPLOYMENT%20 OF%20IRAQI%20CHEMICAL%20AGENTS%20DURIN G%20THE%20PERSIAN%20GULF%20WAR.htm>.

39 Andreas Zumach, "The Secret List of the Arms Dealers—Saddam's Business Partners," *Die Tageszeitung* 17 December 2002.

40 Representative Henry B. Gonzalez (TX-20), "Kissinger Associates, BNL, and Iraq," the Congressional Record <www.fas.org/spp/starwars/congress/ 1991/h910502g.htm>.

41 "Appendix B—The Glaspie–Hussein Transcript" in Phyllis Bennis and Michel Moushabeck, eds., *Beyond the Storm: A Gulf Crisis Reader* (Northampton: Olive Branch Press, 1991).

42 Phyllis Bennis, *Challenging Empire: How People, Governments and the UN Defy US Power* (Northampton: Olive Branch Press, 2006).

43 ICRC, "Principles of International Law Recognized in the Charter of the Nüremberg Tribunal and in the Judgment of the Tribunal, 1950" <www.icrc.org/ ihl.nsf/FULL/390?OpenDocument>.

44 Jason Mark, "Small Towns, Big Sacrifices," CBS News, 17 March 2007 <www.cbsnews.com/stories/ 2007/03/16/opinion/main2578529.shtml>.

45 Ibid.

46 Guy Raz, "Drop in Black Military Recruits Coincides with War," NPR, 7 May 2007.

47 Lizette Alvarez, "Army Effort to Enlist Hispanics Draws Recruits, and Criticism," *New York Times* 9 February 2006.

48 For some of their stories, see <kdka.com/local/ military.signing.bonuses.2.571660.html> and <www.youtube.com/watch?v=x5zUPS_UREg>.

49 Sig Christenson, "Texas is Top State for Army Recruiting," *San Antonio Express-News* 23 January 2008 <www.mysanantonio.com/news/military/stories/MYSA0 12308.03A.Texasrecruits.296e3ef.html>.

50 Eric Schmitt, "Pentagon Contradicts General on Iraq Occupation Force's Size," *New York Times* 28 February 2003.

51 Scott Horton, "Providing Accountability for Private Military Contractors: Testimony before the House Judiciary Committee on June 19, 2007," *Harper's* 19 June 2007.

52 Appeal for Redress <www.appealforredress.org/ index.php>.

53 Le Moyne College and Zogby International, "U.S. Troops in Iraq: 72% Say End War in 2006," 28 February 2006 <www.zogby.com/news/readnews.dbm?id=1075>.

54 RAND Corporation, "One In Five Iraq and Afghanistan Veterans Suffer from PTSD or Major Depression," news release, 17 April 2008 <rand.org/news/press/2008/04/17/>.

55 Marjorie Cohn, *Cowboy Republic: Six Ways the Bush Gang Has Defied the Law* (Sausalito, CA: PoliPoint Press, 2007).

56 Condoleezza Rice and Robert Gates, "What We Need Next in Iraq," *Washington Post* 13 February 2008.

57 State of the Union address, 23 January 1980, President Jimmy Carter <www.jimmycarterlibrary.org/ documents/speeches/su80jec.phtml>.

58 National Security Directive 54, 15 January 1991

<www.washingtonpost.com/wp-srv/inatl/longterm/
fogofwar/docdirective.htm>.

59 "President Discusses Iraq in Press Conference,"
Excerpts from the Press Conference by President George
W. Bush, 7 November 2002 <www.whitehouse.gov/
news/releases/2002/11/20021107-7.html>.

60 BBC, Transcript of Blair's Iraq Interview, 6 February
2003 <news.bbc.co.uk/2/hi/programmes/newsnight/
2732979.stm>.

61 "Top Bush Officials Say Iraq Not in Compliance with
UN," GlobalSecurity.com, 19 January 2003
<www.globalsecurity.org/wmd/library/news/iraq/2003/
iraq-030119-usia01.htm>.

62 "Powell Says NATO Resolution Shows Support for
U.N. on Iraq," GlobalSecurity.com, 22 November 2002
<www.globalsecurity.org/wmd/library/news/iraq/2002/
iraq-021122-usia01.htm>.

63 Jim Garamone, "Americans Quiz Rumsfeld on Radio
Call-in Show," American Forces Press Service
<www.defenselink.mil/news/newsarticle.aspx?id=42501>.

64 Dilip Hiro, "The Oil Grab that Went Awry," *Asia
Times* 27 September 2007 <www.atimes.com/atimes/
Middle_East/II27Ak01.html>.

65 Graham Paterson, "Fed Veteran Greenspan Lambasts
George W. Bush on Economy," *Sunday Times* (London) 16
September 2007.

66 Peter Grier, "Is It All About Oil?" *Christian Science
Monitor* 16 October 2002.

67 Sarah Anderson, "Harry Truman Wouldn't Stand for
It," *St. Louis Post-Dispatch* 2 March 2006.

68 Calculated by Sarah Anderson at the Institute for Policy
Studies based on data in company proxy statements filed with
the Securities and Exchange Commission. Includes salary,
bonus, non-equity incentive plan compensation, perks, above-

market earnings on deferred compensation, and the grant date value of stock and options awards. Sample includes CEOs of the top 30 publicly traded defense contractors that have at least 10 percent of their revenues from defense.

69 All figures calculated by Sarah Anderson at the Institute for Policy Studies, based on Department of Defense, Defense Finance, and Accounting Services and corporate proxy statements. Note: due to changes in reporting requirements, compensation figures for 2006 are not directly comparable to previous years.

70 GAO-08-467SP, "Assessments of Selected Weapons Programs."

71 Anderson, "Harry Truman."

72 Ibid.

73 CNN, "Poll: War Opposition Reaches High Despite Reports of Less Violence," 9 November 2007 <www.cnn.com/2007/POLITICS/11/08/war.poll/index.html>.

74 Douglas Jehl, "Holy War Lured Saudis as Rulers Looked Away," *New York Times* 27 December 2001.

75 Andrew Kohut, "More Say Iraq War Hurts Fight Against Terrorism," the Pew Research Center for the People and the Press, 21 July 2005 <people-press.org/reports/pdf/251.pdf>.

76 Gen. Anthony Zinni, USMC (Ret.), Remarks at CDI Board of Directors Dinner, 12 May 2004 <www.cdi.org/program/document.cfm?DocumentID=2208&from_page=../index.cfm>.

77 Dana Priest, "Iraq New Terror Breeding Ground," *Washington Post* 14 January 2005.

78 Douglas Jehl, "Iraq May Be Prime Place for Training of Militants, C.I.A. Report Concludes," *New York Times* 22 June 2005.

79 International Institute for Strategic Studies, "Iraq War Has Accelerated Al Qaida Recruitment," Reuters, 25 May 2004.

80 Frank Gregory and Paul Wilkinson, "Riding Pillion for Tackling Terrorism Is a High-Risk Policy," ISP/NSC Briefing Paper 05/01, "Security, Terrorism and the UK," Chatham House, July 2005.

81 Bryan Bender, "Study Cites Seeds of Terror in Iraq," *Boston Globe* 17 July 2005.

82 James Bennet, "Spilled Blood Is Seen as Bond That Draws 2 Nations Closer," *CounterPunch* 13 September 2001.

83 Haaretz Service & Reuters, "Report: Netanyahu Says 9/11 Terror Attacks Good for Israel," *Ha'aretz* 16 April 2008 <www.haaretz.com/hasen/spages/975574.html>.

84 "Amnesty International, "Shielded From Scrutiny," 4 November 2002.

85 Human Rights Watch, "Jenin–IDF Military Operations," 3 May 2002.

86 Gary Eason, "Analysis: Asymmetric Warfare," BBC, 1 April 2003.

87 AP, "U.S. Employs Israeli Tactics in Iraq," 13 December 2003.

88 Eason, "Analysis."

89 Rahul Mahajan, reported in "Dual Occupations," US Campaign to End the Israeli Occupation <endtheoccupation.org/article.php?id=314>.

90 AP, "U.S. Employs Israeli Tactics."

91 Amy Goodman, "Manhunt in Iraq: Israel Trains U.S. Assassination Squads," *Democracy Now!* 9 December 2003.

92 Chris McGreal, "Facility 1391: Israel's Secret Prison," *Guardian* 14 November 2003.

93 Gulnoza Saidazimova, "Iran/Iraq: Trade Flow Increases, But Mostly From Tehran to Baghdad," RFE/RL, 4 March 2008.

94 Dafna Linzer, "Troops Authorized to Kill Iranian Operatives in Iraq," *Washington Post* 26 February 2007.

95 Julian Borger and Ian Black, "US Strikes on Iran Predicted as Tension Rises over Arms Smuggling and

Nuclear Fears," *Guardian* 15 September 2007.

96 Ambassador Crocker and General Petraeus's remarks to Senate Foreign Relations Committee, 11 September 2007.

97 Mark Mazzetti, Steven Lee Myers, and Thom Shanker, "Questions Linger on Scope of Iran's Threat in Iraq," *New York Times* 27 April 2008.

98 Ann Scott Tyson, "US Weighing Readiness for Military Action Against Iran," *Washington Post* 26 April 2008.

99 AP, "CIA Director Hayden Says Iran Wants Americans in Iraq Killed," 30 April 2008 <www.foxnews.com/story/0,2933,353509,00.html>.

100 Agence France Presse, "Hamas are Iran's Proxy Warriors: Rice," 30 April 2008 <www.arabia.msn.com/channels/msnnews/article.aspx?CatID=2&ID=485370&S=Hl>.

101 Glenn Kessler and P. Slevin, "Abdullah: Foreign Oppose Attack; Jordanian King to Urge Bush to Focus on Peace in Mideast, Not Invasion of Iraq," *Washington Post* 1 August 2002.

102 Peter C. Valenti, "Middle East: Axis of Paralysis," *World Press Review* 13 March 2003 <www.worldpress.org/Mideast/986.cfm>.

103 Sue Pleming, "Arab World Sees U.S. in Poor Light, Poll Shows," Reuters, 14 April 2008.

104 Tyler Marshall and Paul Watson, "Afghans Teeter on Edge," *Los Angeles Times* 17 September 2001.

105 Salim Lone, "It Wasn't a Bomb But US Policy that Destroyed the UN Hopes in Iraq," *Guardian* 20 August 2004.

106 UN press briefing by Lakhdar Brahimi, special advisor to the secretary-general for Iraq, Baghdad, 2 June 2005 <www.un.org/apps/news/infocus/iraq/infocusnews.asp?NewsID=751&sID=9>.

107 Colin Powell, interview with Aziz Fahmy, Middle

East Broadcasting Center, 2 June 2004 <www.state.gov/
secretary/former/powell/remarks/33104.htm>.

108 Lone, "It Wasn't a Bomb."

109 US Department of State, *Country Reports on Human
Rights Practices 2002* <www.state.gov/g/drl/rls/
hrrpt/2002/>. Cited in Erik Leaver and Sara Johnson, "A
Coalition of Weakness," Foreign Policy in Focus, 24 March
2003 <www.fpif.org/pdf/reports/PRhr.pdf>. Freedom
House ratings also cited in Leaver and Johnson.

110 AP, "In Basra, Violence is a Tenth of What It was
Before British Pullback, General Says," *International Herald
Tribune* 15 November 2007.

111 Iraq Index, Brookings Institution, 31 March 2008
<www.brookings.edu/saban/~/media/Files/Centers/Sab
an/Iraq%20Index/index20080331.pdf>.

112 Pew Research Center, "A Year After Iraq War," 16
March 2004 <people-press.org/reports/display.php
3?ReportID=206>.

113 BBC, "View of U.S. Global Role 'Worse'," 23 January
2007 <news.bbc.co.uk/2/hi/americas/ 6286755.stm>. The
25 countries polled were Argentina, Australia, Brazil, Chile,
China, Egypt, France, Germany, Great Britain, Hungary, India,
Indonesia, Italy, Kenya, Lebanon, Mexico, Nigeria,
Philippines, Poland, Portugal, Russia, South Korea, Turkey,
United Arab Emirates, and the United States.

114 Zogby International/UPI, "UPI Poll: Iraq War
Hurts U.S. Reputation," 24 July 2007
<www.upi.com/Zogby/UPI_Polls/2007/07/24/upi_poll
_iraq_war_hurts_us_reputation/8013/>.

115 Ann Gildroy and Michael O'Hanlon, "How This
Can End," *Washington Post* 16 April 2008.

116 Kim Ghattas, "White House Hopefuls Lay Out Iraq
Plans," BBC, 20 March 2008 <news.bbc.co.uk/2/hi/
americas/7306018.stm>.

117 "Letter from Iraqi Parliamentarians Concerning the MNF Renewal: April 2007," English translation by Global Policy Forum <www.globalpolicy.org/security/issues/iraq/document/2007/042007unletterenglish.pdf>.

118 Stephen Farrell and Robert F. Worth, "Maliki Tries to Rally Arabs Behind Iraq," *New York Times* 23 April 2008.

119 Reese Ehrlich, "Report: U.S. Sponsoring Kurdish Guerilla Attacks Inside Iran," *Democracy Now!* 27 March 2007.

120 Jonathan Weisman, "War Funding Bill Will Put Pelosi's Strength to the Test," *Washington Post* 20 April 2008.

121 Breffni O'Rourke, "British Think Tank Says Iraq Conflict Has Strengthened Al-Qaeda," Radio Free Europe/Radio Liberty, 26 May 2004 <www.globalsecurity.org/wmd/library/news/iraq/2004/05/iraq-040526-rferl01.htm>.

122 Peter Slevin, "U.S. Renounced Its Support of New Tribunal for War Crimes," *Washington Post* 7 May 2002.

123 AP, "In Basra, Violence is a Tenth of What it was Before British Pullback, General Says," 15 November 2007.

124 ABC News, 19 March 2008.

125 Lizette Alvarez, "Army Giving More Waivers in Recruiting," *New York Times* 14 February 2007.

126 <pol.moveon.org/iraq/recession_reports.html>.

127 Jonathan S. Landay and John Walcott, "Pentagon Institute Calls Iraq War 'a Major Debacle' With Outcome 'in Doubt,'" *McClatchy Newspapers* 17 April 2008.

129 Alan Wirzbicki, "Deployments in Iraq Mean Fewer Firefighters," *Boston Globe* 5 June 2008.

130 <www.citiesforpeace.org>.

RESOURCES

Books

Ahmad, Eqbal, with David Barsamian. *Confronting Empire*. Boston: South End Press, 2000.

Ahmad, Eqbal. *The Selected Writings of Eqbal Ahmad*. New York: Columbia University Press, 2006.

Ali, Tariq. *Bush in Babylon: The Recolonisation of Iraq*. London: Verso Books, 2005.

Allawi, Ali A. *The Occupation of Iraq: Winning the War, Losing the Peace*. New Haven: Yale University Press, 2007.

Arnove, Anthony. *Iraq Under Siege: The Deadly Impact of Sanctions and War*. Boston: South End Press, 2000.

Bennis, Phyllis. *Before and After: US Foreign Policy and the War on Terrorism*. Northampton: Olive Branch Press, 2002.

———. *Challenging Empire: How People, Governments, and the UN Defy US Power*. Northampton: Olive Branch Press, 2006.

Bennis, Phyllis, and Michel Moushabeck, eds. *Beyond the Storm: A Gulf Crisis Reader*. Northampton: Olive Branch Press, 1991.

Chandrasekaran, Rajiv. *Imperial Life in the Emerald City*. New York: Vintage, 2007.

Chomsky, Noam. *Hegemony or Survival: America's Quest for Global Dominance*. New York: Henry Holt, 2003.

———. *Rogue States: The Rule of Force in World Affairs*. Boston, South End Press, 2000.

Cockburn, Patrick. *The Occupation: War and Resistance in Iraq*. London: Verso, 2006.

Cohn, Marjorie. *Cowboy Republic: Six Ways the Bush Gang Has Defied the Law*. Sausalito: PoliPoint Press, 2007.

Fallows, James. *Blind into Baghdad*. New York: Vintage, 2006.

Fanon, Frantz. *The Wretched of the Earth*. New York: Grove Press, 1961, 2004.

Flanders, Laura. *Blue Grit: True Democrats Take Back Politics from the Politicians*. New York: Penguin Press, 2007.

Goodman, Amy, and David Goodman. *Static: Government Liars, Media Cheerleaders and the People Who Fight Back*. New York: Hyperion, 2006.

Hayden, Tom. *Ending the War in Iraq*. New York: Akashic Books, 2007.

Hersh, Seymour. *Chain of Command: The Road from 9/11 to AbuGhraib*. New York: HarperCollins, 2004

Horne, Alistair. *A Savage War of Peace: Algeria 1954–1962*. New York: New York Review Books, 2006.

Isikoff, Michael, and David Corn. *Hubris: The Inside Story of Spin, Scandal, and the Selling of the Iraq War*. New York: Three Rivers Press, 2007.

Johnson, Chalmers. *Nemesis: The Last Days of the American Republic*. New York: Metropolitan Books, 2006.

————. *The Sorrows of Empire: Militarism, Secrecy and the End of the Republic*. New York: Metropolitan Books, 2004.

Juhasz, Antonia. *The Tyranny of Oil: The World's Most Powerful Industry—And What We Must Do to Stop It*. New York: HarperCollins, 2008 forthcoming.

————. *The Bush Agenda: Invading the World, One Economy at a Time*. New York: HarperCollins, 2006.

Khalidi, Rashid. *Resurrecting Empire: Western Footprints and America's Perilous Path in the Middle East*. Boston: Beacon Press, 2005.

Klein, Naomi. *The Shock Doctrine: The Rise of Disaster Capitalism*. New York: Metropolitan Books, 2007.

Mamdani, Mahmood. *Good Muslim, Bad Muslim: America, the Cold War and the Roots of Terror*. New York: Doubleday, 2004.

Miller, T. Christian. *Blood Money: Wasted Billions, Lost Lives, and Corporate Greed in Iraq*. New York: Back Bay Books, 2007.

Murray, Andrew, and Lindsey German. *Stop the War: The*

Story of Britain's Biggest Mass Movement. London: Bookmarks Publications, 2005.

Packer, George. *The Assassins' Gate: America in Iraq*. New York: Farrar, Straus and Giroux, 2006.

Pemberton, Miriam, and William D. Hartung. *Lessons from Iraq: Avoiding the Next War*. Boulder and London: Paradigm Publishers, 2008.

Phillips, David. *Losing Iraq: Inside the Postwar Reconstruction Fiasco*. New York: Westview Press, 2005.

Prados, John. *Hoodwinked: The Documents That Reveal How Bush Sold Us a War*. New York: The New Press, 2004.

Ricks, Thomas E. *Fiasco: The American Military Adventure in Iraq*. New York: Penguin Press, 2006.

Scahill, Jeremy. *Blackwater: The Rise of the World's Most Powerful Mercenary Army*. New York: Nation Books, 2007.

Shadid, Anthony. *Night Draws Near: Iraq's People in the Shadow of America's War*. New York: Henry Holt & Co., 2005.

Sökmen, Müge Gürsöy, ed. *World Tribunal on Iraq: Making the Case Against War*. Northampton: Olive Branch Press, 2008.

Stiglitz, Joseph E., and Linda J. Bilmes. *The Three Trillion Dollar War: The True Cost of the Iraq Conflict*. New York: W. W. Norton and Company, 2008.

Vanaik, Achin, ed. *Selling US Wars*. Northampton: Olive Branch Press, 2007.

Woodward, Bob. *Plan of Attack*. New York: Simon and Schuster, 2004.

———. *State of Denial: Bush at War, Part III*. New York: Simon and Schuster, 2006.

Wright, Col. Ann (ret.), and Susan Dixon. *Dissent: Voices of Conscience—Government Insiders Speak Out Against the War in Iraq*. Kihei: Koa Books, 2008.

Reports

Belasco, Amy. "The Cost of Iraq, Afghanistan and other Global

War on Terror Operations Since 9/11." Congressional Research Service Report for Congress. 8 February 2008.

Institute for Policy Studies and Foreign Policy in Focus. "The Iraq Quagmire: The Mounting Costs of the Iraq War." 31 August 2005. <www.classic.ips-dc.org/iraq/quagmire/>

The Iraq Study Group Report ("Baker-Hamilton Commission"). 6 December 2006. <www.usip.org/isg/iraq_study_group_report/report/1206/index.html>

Organizations

US:

American Friends Service Committee (www.afsc.org)
Appeal for Redress (www.appealforredress.org)
Black Voices for Peace (www.blacksforpeace.org)
Cities for Peace (www.citiesforpeace.org)
Code Pink (www.codepink4peace.org)
Institute for Policy Studies (www.ips-dc.org)
Iraq Veterans Against the War (www.ivaw.org)
Middle East Research and Education Project (www.merip.org)
Military Families Speak Out (www.mfso.org)
Peace Action (www.peace-action.org)
Service Women's Action Network (servicewomen.org/projects.shtml)
United for Peace and Justice (www.unitedforpeace.org). (Note: United for Peace and Justice is the largest US peace coalition, with over 1,450 member organizations. Most of those listed here are members of UFPJ.)
US Campaign to End Israeli Occupation (www.endtheoccupation.org)

US Labor Against the War (www.uslaboragainstwar.org)
War Resisters League (www.warresisters.org)
Win Without War (www.winwithoutwarus.org)

CANADA:

Alternatives (www.alternatives.ca)
Canadians Against War (www.canadiansagainstwar.org)
Canadian Council for International Cooperation
(www.ccic.ca/e/home/index.shtml)
Canadian Peace Alliance
(www.acp-cpa.ca/en/index.html)
Canadian Voice of Women for Peace
(home.ca.inter.net/~vow/)
Inter Pares (www.interpares.ca)

UK:

Iraq Body Count (www.iraqbodycount.org)
Military Families Against the War (www.mfaw.org.uk)
Network for Peace (www.networkforpeace.org.uk)
Stop the War Coalition (www.stopwar.org.uk)

THE NETHERLANDS:

Transnational Institute (www.tni.org)